D1796429

Making All Things New in Old Town

Making All Things New in Old Town

Curtis Kemper Norman

ARCHDEACON BOOKS
Hoover, Alabama

ARCHDEACON BOOKS
Hoover, Alabama 35244

ARCHDEACON BOOKS is the publishing imprint of WOODY NORMAN LLC. Its purpose is to provide publishing services and editing advice for first-time and continuing authors.

Distributed through Ingram Content Group.

Published in the United States of America
WOODY NORMAN LLC, Hoover, Alabama

First published in 2018
Paperback

Cover – Pencil Drawing
St. John's Episcopal Church
Courtesy of the Vestry
St. John's Episcopal Church
Saginaw, Michigan

ISBN-13: 978-1-949422-95-5
Hardback Edition

Contents

Preface

As one who grew up in the Episcopal Church, I have become well acquainted with the different witticisms Episcopalians love to tell about themselves. For example, the promise of Heaven could be denied to the Episcopalian who mistakenly uses a salad fork for the main course. Or, when one rearranges the letters E-P-I-S-C-O-P-A-L without adding or subtracting any, it comes out "Pepsi Cola."

And, once upon a time, we would say with a chuckle the purpose of the altar rail was to separate the Republicans from the one Democrat, or vice-versa, depending on the region of the country.

There was an era in my lifetime when Episcopalians could joke about political affinities. But such is not the case any longer. Since my ordination to the diaconate in 2001 and priesthood in 2002, there have been times when parishioners attempted to find out how I vote. Why? If I can be labeled according to the American two-party political dualism, certain parishioners can then decide how they feel about me and whether or not they wish to attend the church I serve.

But the challenge they soon discover is this: I do not worship at the altar of American politics. My Bible does not translate Psalm 121 to say: *I lift my eyes to Capitol Hill -- from where will my help come?*

This form of idolatry is not unique to the Episcopal Church. In my estimation, all of 21st Century American Christianity is struggling to find its footing. How is the Church supposed to embody "... *thy Kingdom come, thy will be done, on earth as it is in heaven*"? Too many strands of Jesus followers are using the Democrat or Republican party as a proxy to accomplish what only the Church can do.

The 2016 Presidential Election did not divide the United States of America. Instead, it revealed how divided we are. To me, this is further proof that salvation comes not from Washington, a candidate, or a party. And since that is the case, the Church should not succumb to the temptation to outsource its mission to political action committees. American Christianity needs to again trust in the temporal and eternal life which comes from faith in the God revealed in Jesus of Nazareth.

What follows in this book are homiletic attempts to help myself and my congregation discover God in our midst and be on the lookout for how the Holy Spirit is brooding chaos into order.

***

The homilies in this compilation break no theological ground (I hope). They are simply part of my attempt to communicate the Gospel of Jesus Christ to the people of St. John's Episcopal Church in Saginaw, Michigan, USA in the 21st Century.

The reader will notice my homilies are not long in duration. There is an old saying in the Episcopal Church that there is no salvation after twelve minutes. On average, my homilies run about eight or nine minutes. As important as I believe the preached word is in the context of the liturgy, I prepare and execute with the idea that the homily/sermon is simply a part of the liturgy.

Another guiding principle for homily preparation is rooted in my eight years as an editor, reporter, and (sometimes) announcer at KRLD, the CBS Radio news affiliate in Dallas, Texas. People will only give you so much time to hear what you have to say; you have to be efficient with your language. If you are going to speak, then you actually need to say something (one can preach for fifteen or eighteen minutes and not say that much). This is not to contend I accomplish these goals in any or all of my homilies, but I do try.

Only on rare occasions do I use a direct quotation from a theologian, and such instances are footnoted in the text. I try to write my messages without books surrounding my laptop. In my opinion, while preachers need to have a strong theological foundation, sermons/homilies are not academic lectures. Thus, and may be evident by the way the words sit on the page in this book, I endeavor to write for the "ear" and not the "eye."

In 2017, I learned via book, article, video, social media post(s) or podcast from the following:

Richard Rohr, NT Wright, Pope Benedict XVI, Brene Brown, John R. Donahue SJ, Stephen Prothero, Max Lucado, Peter Enns, Jim Gettel, Brian McLaren, Timothy Keller, Ravi Zacharias, Jonathan Sacks, Michael Curry, aish.com, Crackers and Grape Juice, The Bible for Normal People, The Bible Project, On Being with Krista Tippett, Rob Bell, Quick to Listen, The Accidental Talmudist, Fleming Rutledge, Nyasha Junior, Becca Stevens, Lisa Sharon Harper, Jordan Ware, Paul Zahl, The Michigan Catholic, Christianity Today, The Living Church, Priest Pulse, Miroslav Volf, James Martin SJ, Rachel Held Evans, Justin Welby, Dwight Longenecker, Rod Dreher, and countless others.

Whether I agreed or disagreed with what I read or heard, it all made me think as I prepared my homilies.

JANUARY

New Journeys

Homily for January 8, 2017
First Sunday in a New Parish

Today we begin a new journey. Several journeys, in fact.

As your new rector, I am excited about what God is calling St. John's to be at this time, in this space, and outside these walls. It will be a lot of work for all of us. But it is going to be fun! It will be meaningful and life-changing.

In addition, a new journey begins this morning (at the 10:30 service) for the Fergin family. Liam will be baptized. Rachelle, Brad, and the godparents will promise to do their very best, with God's grace, to help Liam grow into the full stature of Christ. And all of us will promise to do all in our power to support Liam in his life in Christ. We are not merely spectators; we are participants.

But to know where God is leading us, we need to understand how God has been faithful to us in the past. So, as we embark on these new journeys, which merge with the journeys we are already on, it is important to remember where these journeys have their beginning.

Our Gospel writer, Matthew, invites us this morning to the Jordan River where Jesus' cousin, John the Baptist, is… well… baptizing.

Now, each of the Gospel accounts has a different emphasis when it comes to talking about Jesus' baptism. In John's Gospel… NOT John the Baptist; it is a different John… we learn that Jesus' baptism occurred at a place called Bethany beyond the Jordan.

When we think about the geography in first century Palestine, what is now the nation state of Israel… we have the Sea of Galilee to the north, which empties south into the Jordan River, which empties south into the Dead Sea.

Bethany beyond the Jordan is like an intersection… it is located roughly near where the Jordan River empties into the Dead Sea. The Dead Sea is about 1,320 feet below sea level, making it the lowest place on earth. We are going to need to remember this.

Back to Matthew's Gospel… which tells us something about Jesus' baptism that the other three gospels do not. In today's gospel lesson, we find ourselves in the middle of the Jordan River… where John has been screaming at people to repent, turn around, re-think our lives… because the kingdom of heaven is near.

Heaven and earth have merged in the person of Jesus of Nazareth… Jesus is the intersection between the human and the divine… and Jesus invites us into this intersection.

But much to the astonishment of John the Baptist, Jesus presents himself for baptism. This does not make sense to John. In his mind, Jesus is superior… and he, John, is inferior. So it would only make sense for Jesus to baptize John, right?

This is called dualistic thinking.

Jesus is good, John is bad.

Taken to another level, God is good, humanity is bad. And for humanity to "reach" God … and we might even say "before" humanity can experience God, we have to clean up our act first. In this frame of thought, in this dualistic way of thinking, there is no way humanity can make itself acceptable to God until we achieve moral purity.

And while this may sound archaic to the Episcopal understanding of Jesus… because it is… there are well-meaning Christians around the world who view baptism in this light. To some, baptism is seen ONLY as an act on a path to moral perfection so that we may punch our ticket to heaven. For some, baptism has implications for the afterlife only.

But I do not see it that way.

If baptism… if Christianity… is only about going to heaven after we die (and I certainly believe that is a huge part of God's promise to us, do not hear me saying anything different)… but if Christianity is only an escape-hatch from the sinful here-and-now just so we can go to heaven after we die… then we fail to understand the full meaning of baptism… and we place limits on the Resurrection-life offered to us by Jesus for the here-and-now.

I say this because we see in Matthew's gospel today that Jesus offered himself for baptism. Through his incarnation and baptism, God comes to us in the person of Jesus of Nazareth on our level… he is with us in the waters of baptism… he meets us literally and figuratively at the lowest place on earth, the lowest places in our lives… and it is there where Jesus begins to journey with us.

Today, as we continue our journeys, and begin some new ones, let us recognize that God is with us in Jesus… he has been walking with us already, even though we may not have noticed… and he will continue with us on our journeys.

What Are You Looking For?

Homily for January 15, 2017

I heard a story[1] recently about a journey by a village wise-man. Let me be clear, this is NOT one of the Magi who visited the toddler Jesus on what we call the Feast of the Epiphany. This is more a story of folklore.

In any case, the wise-man decided one day to take a walk in the vast woods outside his village. It became dark… and not just dark, but foggy. So, after a lengthy stroll, he decided to head back to his village. But at a key spot along the way home, the wise-man turned in the opposite direction from which he was supposed to go.

Instead of arriving at his village, the darkness and fog steered the wise-man to a military outpost. The garrison had a wall around it about ten-feet high. And there was a soldier on top of the wall, directly above him.

The soldier called down to the wise-man: "Who are you? And what are you doing here?"

The wise-man paused for a moment, looked up, and said to the soldier: "What?"

The soldier shouted down louder: "Who are you? And what are you doing here?"

The wise-man paused again, scratched his head, and said to the soldier: "How much do they pay you?"

---

[1] Opening story heard from a podcast hosted by Rob Bell

The solider said: "What?"

The wise-man repeated his question: "How much does your commanding officer pay you?"

The soldier said: "50-denarri a week."

The wise-man responded: "I'll pay you twice that, if you come back with me to my village and, every day, ask me those two questions."

***

Who are we? And what are we doing here?

***

When I hear this story in light of today's gospel passage, I am reminded how valuable probing questions can be.

We again find ourselves in the presence of John the Baptist. On two Sundays in Advent, John brought to mind the concept of expectation. He raised our awareness about the Messiah who was and is coming into the world. And I believe, on some level, John had to adjust at least a few of the expectations he had projected onto Jesus.

That is the thing about expectation.

Cynics all too easily say that expectation leads to disappointment.

But for people of faith, expectation leads to epiphany. When we adopt a posture of receptivity, when we make ourselves vulnerable, God reveals God's self. But such a revelation may rarely look exactly like that which we construct in our minds. And the unexpected discovery is not disappointment; it is epiphany.

There are two wonderful, focused, insightful questions in today's gospel that we are invited to ponder. The first comes off the lips of Jesus. John the Baptist says out loud that Jesus is the Lamb of God who has come into the world to close the gap between the divine and human. Two of John's disciples hear this proclamation. And these disciples of John approach Jesus… and when Jesus notices they are now following him, Jesus asks them: "What are you looking for?"

What are you looking for?

What are we looking for?

When we approach Jesus in our daily lives, what are we looking for? Are we seeking a savior akin to a genie in a bottle, wanting that genie to cater to our every whim? Do we seek a care-free existence? Is faith about what I want, when I want it? And if God does not make my life turn out the way I have it planned, then do I have a need for God we meet in Scripture? Do I even know the God of Scripture?

Or is there something more to following Jesus, something that takes us to places we do not necessarily want to go, at first?

These new followers of Jesus respond to Jesus with a question of their own: "Rabbi, where are you staying?"

And this is not simply: What's your address? Where's your church? (because Jesus' church doesn't exist at this point) This is not a question limited to physical proximity.

This is a much deeper question: Where do you abide? What are you about? What does it mean for you to be the Lamb of God? What does it mean for us to be your followers?

Jesus offers a simple answer to the question. It is simple. But it is not easy. When Jesus is asked where he is staying, what he is about, what does it mean to follow him, Jesus says:

"Come and see."

Come and see.

As we embark on a new season of following Jesus… as we endeavor to discern together what it is God has in store for us at St. John's, both individually and collectively… we need to spend some time pondering questions… and allow space for Epiphany to unfold.

Who are we? What are we doing here? What are we looking for? Where does Jesus abide?

And the best way for us to faithfully engage these questions is to come and see.

Withdraw and (re) Engage

Homily for January 22, 2017

Did Jesus ever have a bad day? I mean, apart from Good Friday.

I wonder from time-to-time if our culture paints too antiseptic a portrait of Jesus… a happy-go-lucky savior in a clean, white, flowing robe… basking in sun-drenched blue skies… surrounded by rainbows and unicorns. To paraphrase a well-worn saying: are we so heavenly-minded about Jesus that he is no earthly good?

Today's gospel lesson begins with Jesus learning that his cousin, John the Baptist… yes, here he is AGAIN… John the Baptist has been arrested.

What goes through our minds… how do we feel physically, emotionally, and spiritually… when someone we are close to… someone we know and love... finds themselves in a difficult, life-threatening situation?

Why would Jesus not feel the same as we do? Was Jesus confused? Did he feel inadequate? Helpless?

We know why John the Baptist was arrested. His first words recorded in Matthew's gospel were: "Repent, for the kingdom of heaven has come near."

Rethink your life. Allow God's way of being to permeate your existence.

With these words and their import, John drew quite the following. John was a popular religious figure of his day. It is probably why the gospel writers go to great lengths to have John say he is **not** the long-awaited Messiah. John always points away from himself and to Jesus.

John's preaching became personal... maybe a bit too personal... for Herod Antipas, the first-century ruler of Galilee and Perea. John called this government official on the carpet because Herod divorced his wife to take his brother's wife. And if that was not seedy enough, Herod had eyes for his step-daughter/niece.

John believed that the most visible politician in his region should be ethical, of sound character, and set good examples. I think we can faithfully infer from the text that John cared for Herod and others in power... and that John cared even more for the people over whom the politicians had influence.

Herod certainly liked to listen to what John had to say, which makes me wonder if the two ever sat down for long, one-on-one conversations.

But when John's rebuke of Herod's sins became too much for Herodias... Herod's new wife and former sister-in-law... out of her apparent insecurity, or maybe even shame and embarrassment of subjugation, Herodias demanded that Herod arrest John.

Like sands through the hourglass, so are the days of our lives.

With two thousand years of reflection, we know how John's story ended: capital punishment.

Herod got drunk at his own birthday party... his niece/step-daughter danced for him... Herod liked it and made a promise in front of all his guests to give the dancer anything she wanted. Herodias influenced her daughter's decision... so Herodias got what she wanted: John's head on a platter.

Yes, we know how it all ended for John the Baptist.

But I think Jesus knew how it was going to end, shortly after John was arrested. Matthew tells us that when John the Baptist was taken into custody, Jesus withdrew. Jesus withdrew to Galilee. Jesus embarked on an outer journey likely in order to help him process an inner journey.

When John was arrested, life became intense for Jesus. Jesus could see that just as the curtain was closing on John's ministry, his ministry was in its opening act.

But before Jesus called his first disciples… before he became known as the "light of the world" … Jesus had to acknowledge the darkness.

Jesus had to withdraw… something he would do often in his public ministry (Luke 5:16).

Jesus had to step back… see things as they are… see evil for what it is… count the costs… come to grips with the fact that John would likely die in prison… and that his own ministry would lose him his life, as well. But where there is death, God creates new life.

There was darkness all around. Yet Jesus knew he was anointed to be God's dawning light to scatter the darkness which enveloped God's people.

And when confronted with this sobering reality, while Matthew does not say it here with words, we can bet that Jesus would pray. Jesus would withdraw from the intensity of his life to connect with God the Father… so that he could again engage with the world around him.

I am not sure how long it took Jesus to get from Nazareth to Galilee… how long it took from the time he learned of John's arrest before he introduced himself to Peter, Andrew, James, and John.

But somewhere in these sentences, Jesus again freely embraced God's call on his life… fully aware of both risk and reward.

We would do well to learn from Jesus when presented with the choice to avoid darkness… or to be God's light.

Jesus withdrew... but he also re-engaged... and the first words he spoke upon re-engagement were the words that got John the Baptist into trouble... but they are also words that bring light into the world... and they are words we are called to speak today.

May God give us the grace to be bold... and proclaim:

Repent, for the kingdom of heaven has come near.

Poor in Spirit

Homily for January 29, 2017

Today is one of those days when we are on "St. John's overload." We had the Celebration of a New Ministry yesterday afternoon, several of you went to the symphony last night, and we have the Annual Meeting this morning.

Lots of activity and information coming our way… and because that is apparently not enough, we are presented with a Gospel passage we could study for the next year.

Jesus begins his Sermon on the Mount. He invites us into God's way of living that is 180-degrees from what we may experience around us… different from what our default behaviors might be.

Each of these Beatitudes… understandings of what it means to be blessed or truly happy… each of them has to be unpacked so that we can experience their depth.

At some point in the near future, we will study the Beatitudes in a Sunday school setting. For now, allow me to offer a brief example.

When Jesus says "Blessed are the poor in spirit," that has little or nothing to do with material wealth… it is an acknowledgement that we need God's help to live as God would have us. On our own, we cannot do what we promise in our Baptismal Covenant:

> persevering in resisting evil,
> seeking and serving Christ in all persons,
> loving our neighbor as ourselves,
> respecting the dignity of every human being.

These tenets of our faith are at risk in our day.

Now is our time as Episcopal Christians to act in the name of the God we know in Jesus.

We must do this, not with arrogance, but humility.

Jesus calls us to be "poor in spirit" … to create space in our lives for God to live in and through us.

If I were to stand up here and tell you: "I'm rich in spirit" … "I've got this God-centered life all figured out" … "I know what to do in every life situation that comes my way" … which is then turned into: "God never gives me more than I can handle" … that would be false. And that is why, when we are asked in the Prayer Book if we'll live as Jesus teaches, our response is: "I will, with God's help."

***

As always, when I read Scripture, I have questions.

What kind of people will we become when we live into Jesus' Beatitudes, when we allow the grace of God to work in us?

What transformation awaits St. John's when we engage even more deeply with our Baptismal Covenant?

How will the Beatitudes raise our awareness of God's activity in the world?

How enlightened will we become, in the proper sense of that word?

One answer to these questions is found in a brief meditation by the late Catholic priest Anthony DeMello. It is from his book *One Minute Wisdom*.

This meditation is titled "Rejection" … and you will hear why. It goes like this:

"What kind of person does Enlightenment produce?"

Said the Master:

"To be public-spirited and belong to no party,
to move without being bound to any given course,
to take things as they come,
have no remorse for the past,
no anxiety for the future,
to move when pushed,
to come when dragged,
to be like a mighty gale,
like a feather in the wind,
like weeds floating on a river,
like a mill stone meekly grinding,
to love all creation equally as heaven and earth are equal to all –
such is the product of Enlightenment."

On hearing these words, one of the younger disciples cried, "This sort of teaching is not for the living but for the dead," and walked away, never to return.

***

To use language from the Apostle Paul, the younger disciple in this meditation views the way of Jesus… the Cross of Christ… as foolishness.

But we trust this journey to be the power and wisdom of God.

How might those around us benefit when we have faith that Jesus' Beatitudes… an awareness of God… and enlightenment by the Holy Spirit… all culminating in the death and resurrection of Jesus… how might we and others be blessed when we trust these things to bring the dead to life?

FEBRUARY

Salt

Homily for February 5, 2017

What does it look like to be the Jesus Movement at St. John's Episcopal Church in Old Town Saginaw, Michigan, in the United States of America, in A.D. 2017?

This morning's gospel lesson is again from Jesus' Sermon on the Mount. Jesus offers an answer to the question I just posed… and not just an answer, but images… because images can often teach us more than will platitudes.

I want us to focus, for the most part, on ONE of the images.

Jesus says his followers are: SALT.

In biblical times, salt was used as currency, for seasoning, preservation, as disinfectant, for ceremonial purposes, and more.

One of my favorite stories from the Bible involving salt is found in Genesis chapter 19. It is a story you probably will not read to your children or grandchildren at bedtime. If you do, we need to talk.

The story involves Lot, the nephew of Abraham, a biblical figure claimed by Judaism, Christianity, and Islam. As the story goes, two angels of the Lord inform Lot that God is going to destroy the twin cities of Sodom and Gomorrah… because the people there failed to show hospitality to strangers.

Given the overall trajectory of Genesis, I tend to believe this story… as a literary device… is about abandoning a false notion of God as persistently angry at humanity… and arriving at a place where we know God as love.

In any case, Lot and his family are hesitant to leave Sodom. Their life was comfortable, if not privileged. The land was fertile, the economy was robust. Still, the angels of the Lord nudge Lot and his family into motion.

On the way out of Sodom, the angels tell them: "Don't look back." But what is the one thing Lot's wife does? She looks back… and she becomes a pillar of salt.

By looking back, Lot's wife reveals that she is consumed with the past. Is she trying to preserve the good old days that really never were? Is she content to stay in the unhealthy complacency of history, unwilling to embrace the future God had in store?

In a larger context, is Lot's wife so convinced that "God is out to get us" that she can never come to understand that "God is for us?"

Salt, in this story, is an image for extreme, destructive preservation.

But that is not how Jesus uses salt in his analogy.

Jesus says we are the salt of the earth. According to some theologians, just as light is needed where there is darkness… salt is needed where there is corruption.

But I would add, it is not enough for us as followers of Jesus to simply stop corruption. We should, at the same time, bring out the good. We are to be salt, not only for the sake of disinfectant, but for seasoning.

We are here not only to combat humanity's Original Sin… we are here to pronounce God's Original Blessing.

***

Another favorite story of mine comes from the Book of Exodus.

Moses, after murdering an Egyptian in a failed attempt to bring about justice for the enslaved Hebrews, has fled to the wilderness. He is struggling to figure out who he is and what his purpose in life is.

Moses notices a bush that is on fire but not being consumed. He knows what should happen when shrubbery is ablaze.

But what should be happening is not. And since Moses is never content to allow the current reality of life to fall short of God's dream, he draws closer to the burning bush to reconcile this in his own mind... and responds.

As Moses approaches a paradox, Moses encounters God, who tells Moses his purpose: You, Moses, are to lead God's people from bondage to freedom... from darkness to light... away from corruption and toward holiness.

In the course of this exchange, Moses asks God what God's name is. What is God's nature and essence? And behind that, why should Moses take his life purpose from this God?

God responds: Y-H-W-H... a name that our Jewish sisters and brothers neither pronounce nor fully write out. After all, how can human letters, how can human language, apprehend God?

Rabbis tell us there are many ways to define Yahweh. We have come to understand the divine name as I AM... or I AM WHO I AM... or I WAS, I AM, I SHALL BE.

God's name speaks to God's eternal BEING.

God did not say: I DID, I DO, I SHALL DO.

God's essence does not begin with DOING... it begins with BEING.

And if all humanity is created in the image of God, then our self-understanding… our self-worth… our purpose in life… begins, not with DOING, but BEING… who we ARE.

***

Jesus says: we ARE the salt of the earth.

May God give us the grace to become who we are.

How NOT to Get Away With Murder

Homily for February 12, 2017

Murder. Anger. Insults. Adultery. Lust. Dismemberment. Hell. Divorce. Unchastity.

Now that Jesus has our attention… what is he trying to tell us?

Today, Jesus brings depth to God's desire for humanity. Following the God we know in Jesus does not begin and end simply with external actions. Following Jesus involves the transformation of our hearts.

In the sentences prior to what we just read, which we actually heard at the end of the Gospel lesson last Sunday, Jesus says he has not come to undo the Law and Prophets of Hebrew Scriptures (portions of what we often call the Old Testament). God did not take on flesh in Jesus to create a new religion. Instead, Jesus has come to fulfill the Scriptures.

That means: when we come to know Jesus, we begin to see what God intends for humanity… and once we see God's desire for humanity, we INCORPORATE that into our own lives, our own communities.

On a macro level, Jesus speaks about the relationship between anger and murder, adultery and divorce, as well as oaths and allegiances. When we hear these categories, we know that Jesus is referencing to a large degree the Ten Commandments which God gave to Israel through Moses… the structure God provided for the community God liberated from a tyrant who did not value their humanity.

Let's go through these briefly… because they will become part of our liturgy during Lent.

From Exodus 20, the Ten Commandments are:

I am the LORD your God, there is no other God but me. Whereas the Greeks, Romans, and other cultures believed in many gods (polytheism), the Jewish people come along and discern: no, there is just one God (monotheism).

Do NOT make yourself any idols (do not create gods with a small 'g')… and we can do that with education, wealth, religious denomination, politics, personal accomplishments or whatever else. I am not saying any of those things are bad, but we have to place them in proper perspective. I always have to smash the small 'g' gods I create.

Do NOT take the LORD's name in vain. And I love this commandment. It really has nothing to do with saying "G-D" … this is more about not attributing to God characteristics that do not belong to God. If I were to stand here and say: "God was upset with the people of New Orleans, so God sent Hurricane Katrina." That is taking the LORD's name in vain.

Remember the Sabbath Day and keep it holy. In one of the creation accounts in Genesis, God takes time to rest and reflect on creation. God is not a workaholic. Are we?

Honor your father and mother. This commandment is not meant for parents to lord over their young children in the home. What if I were to tell you this is meant as instruction for how adults are to relate to their aging parents?

Do NOT murder.

Do NOT commit adultery.

Do NOT steal.

Do NOT bear false witness against your neighbor.

Do NOT covet. I have heard lots of explanations for this commandment. But my favorite is this: do not wish you had somebody else's life. Be thankful for the life God has given you.

***

Notice that the first four commandments have to do with the relationship between humanity and God. We could call those the vertical commandments. The next five commandments deal with human-to-human relationships, and we could call those horizontal commandments.

And when we place a vertical line with a horizontal line, we get a cross. +

The tenth commandment, according to some rabbis I read, is an internal commandment. And that is to say, only you will know how you are interacting with the first nine commandments. And only you will know whether or not you are coveting, if you are thankful for the life God has given you, or if you wish God had done something else with your life.

***

Today, Jesus offers us a way to integrate God's truth found in the Ten Commandments. Let's take just one example.

Jesus says: "You have heard that it was said to those of ancient times, 'You shall not murder; and whoever murders shall be liable to judgment.' But I say to you that if you are angry with a brother or sister, you will be liable to judgment…"

Okay, we can stop right there.

What Jesus is saying is that we can commit murder without actually killing a person. We can cause irreparable damage to others and ourselves merely by the attitudes of our hearts. Death comes in many forms.

Sometimes I wonder if I should read this passage before logging on to social media. The phrase "character assassination" comes to mind.

The remedy to this sin is reconciliation… which is not always desirable. It makes us look weak. And that is not cool in a culture that says "… never let them see you sweat."
But here's the image Jesus provides.

Jesus says when we are offering our gift at the altar… that is to say, when we desire to approach God with the entirety of our being… we are not able to do that completely when we harbor anger against another person created in the image of God.

When we hold on to anger, self-righteousness, pride, inflexibility, the possibility of revenge, we block out God as much as we block out the person who is on the receiving end of our anger. This is not a case of God punishing us for the sin of anger. We punish ourselves… and we take others down with us.

What Jesus would have us do in these situations is “come to terms quickly” with those whom we call opponents.

I am not under any illusion. This is difficult work. Following Jesus is not for the faint of heart. It is for those who allow God to transform their hearts.

Might this be exactly what is needed in our day?

God's Future for St. John's

Homily for February 19, 2017

Today is my seventh Sunday as Rector of St. John's. So, this morning, I want to reflect on conversations I have had with many of you since arriving.

I receive a fair number of questions about the future of St. John's. What is God calling us to DO now that I am your rector?

A couple of weeks ago I spoke from this pulpit about how we are grounded in BEING… and doing grows out of being. What St. John's has done, does, and will do should be a direct result of who we are.

We will not endeavor to be a congregation we are not. We will continue to grow more fully into who we are… liturgically, musically, how we engage the community of Saginaw, and more.

***

If I were to re-word some of the questions coming my way, it might sound like this: "Fr. Curt, what is your VISION for St. John's?"

Simply put, I do NOT have a vision for St. John's. As I have told several of you privately, God has a vision for St. John's. Each of you catches a piece of the vision through prayer… and it is my task to listen to you (while I am listening to God in prayer) in order to hear God's vision… communicate this vision back to you… and together we assemble the puzzle.

Almost everything that I have heard from you thus far has to do with stewardship. We in the Episcopal Church understand that stewardship is not just money.

But make no mistake: I am not afraid to broach this topic from the pulpit, in vestry meetings, or in person. And that is because Jesus spoke about MONEY more than he did about any other single topic. In fact, Jesus talked about MONEY more than Heaven and Hell combined. And do not just take my word for that; check it out for yourselves.

Stewardship includes financial treasure…as much as it is about time and talent.

What you are telling me is that improving financial stewardship at St. John's is a priority… because there are projects like restoring the stained-glass windows and construction of a columbarium which need to become realities.

As I tell you this, I must admit I am not setting a good enough example for you. At this point in our lives, Margaret and I are not tithing (giving ten-percent of our income) to St. John's.

I could offer all sorts of excuses about how we arrived at this point over the past several years. But what I can say is that we are increasing our giving. I ask your prayers for us as we embark on this journey back to the tithe.

One of the temptations I have encountered during this time is to think that whatever small amount I put in the offering plate… small as in comparison to what others might be giving… the temptation is to think that God cannot use that small amount. And if I do not believe God can use what I have to offer, then why even bother giving it?

But we must remember there are plenty of examples in Scripture where something that seems to be inadequate turns out to be exactly what God needs to get a task accomplished.

You are expressing the need to see financial giving increase. And you are also expressing a desire to bolster the St. John's endowment.

Previous generations of St. John's parishioners made it possible for us to benefit today from their giving. We owe it to future generations to have the St. John's endowment work for them. One of the ways that we will make this happen is through planned giving. And we will have more to share on that in the not-too-distant future.

So, just as you are praying for me to improve my family's financial stewardship, I would ask that you prayerfully consider your own giving, as well.

***

Another stewardship topic deals with outreach.

What is God's vision for us to help bring wholeness to God's people in and around Saginaw, Michigan? This is a broad stewardship question which involves time and talent, as well as treasure.

We do much good already. But as all of us know, there is a lot of need in Saginaw… and as much as St. John's has been, is, and should be an anchor in Old Town… there is more need than St. John's alone can handle.

Again, the temptation when there is so much need is to draw back and do nothing. As followers of Jesus, that is not an option for us. We will prayerfully consider what it is that God is calling us to do… as a congregation and through partnerships in the community… and all of that will be rooted in who we are.

***

This morning, as we continue this journey God has us on, I offer not an answer or a direction… but an observation as somebody who pulled into town on December 29.

***

Children who attend Saginaw Public Schools face serious challenges. And that may be an understatement.

We here at St. John's have a lot of people who are in the profession of education… which, I believe, is a calling from God.

Those who are not professional educators are well-educated… which, I believe, should be understood as a gift from God.

When we hold these realities side-by-side… what is God saying to us, both individually and collectively?

As we move into God's future for St. John's… I would like for us as a congregation to hold up these realities in prayer … and I am eager to learn in the coming weeks and months how God speaks to you and to all of us.

MARCH

Ash Wednesday 2017

Homily for March 1, 2017

On this Ash Wednesday, I would like for us to consider what it is we do every day with our hands.

***

Do we fold our hands in prayer?

Wipe away the tears of a loved one?

Gently brush strands of hair out of another's eyes?

Do we pat someone on the back?

Hold hands with someone dear?

Prepare breakfast?

Write, type, or text a note?

Offer a healing touch to someone who is sick?

Have we clapped?

Waved goodbye or hello?

Taken one or both hands off the steering wheel to express disgust at a fellow driver?

Has it been one of those days when we've made a clenched fist?

Do our hands hurt from working… or simply because of age?

Does winter make our hands dry?

***

In a moment, you will be invited forward to receive the imposition of ashes.

As Pam and I take our hands and mark the sign of the cross on your forehead, we will say these words: "Remember that you are dust, and to dust you shall return."

For these words to make any sense, we must look at the first phrase of the prayer used to bless the ashes: "Almighty God, you have created us out of the dust of the earth."

This is a direct reference to the second creation account, Genesis 2:7… ".. the LORD God formed man from the dust of the ground and breathed into his nostrils the breath of life; and the man became a living being." And when this first human came to life, God placed him in the Garden of Eden… and gave him a job. The man began to till and keep the soil; humanity became God's steward for the earth.

The first human was, if you will, a gardener. He worked with his hands.

It seems simple enough. But Hebrew scholars tell us there is much lost in translation.

The Hebrew verbs used in this particular creation account are verbs associated with pottery. So, we are to imagine God sitting at a potter's wheel… God as an artist, forming and crafting, as with hands, the first human being in God's own image… and then breathing life into that first human.

We could say that God has dirt under the fingernails; callouses and blisters on the palms; God is not afraid for God's own hands to be pierced and scarred.

God is not put off by the wear and tear that comes from interacting with humanity.

***

Ash Wednesday is a sober reminder that death is inevitable.

We must allow death (both literal and metaphorical) to have its proper place.

When we try to deny death in its various forms… avoid the reality of a return to the dust… we close off our lives from the peace which comes from knowing that we rest in the hands of a God whose loving touch re-forms, re-crafts, and resurrects.

***

As we embark on our Lenten journeys, what is it that the God who embraces us in Jesus needs to re-form?

What are the barriers we place between ourselves and God that need to be pushed down… so that God can craft us anew?

Where are we in most need of the hands of God… so that we can, in turn, embody the hands of a God who desires to resurrect our communities?

Did God Say?

Homily for March 5, 2017

When our son was in Kindergarten in Texas, his class took a field-trip to a place called Dinosaur World. It is a venue where visitors can, and I quote, "…wander among hundreds of life-sized dinosaurs in a natural setting."

Essentially, it is a low-tech Jurassic Park. And it is fun to watch the kids walk through the woods and see a brontosaurus or T-Rex above or behind the trees… so long as the dinosaurs do not move. And they don't.

But what I found fascinating when I visited Dinosaur World is that there is something pretty interesting across the street from Dinosaur World. You see, Dinosaur World is committed to science. It teaches children that dinosaurs roamed the earth 65-million years ago… and that the earth is more than 4.5-billion years old.

This world view does not sit well with some segments of good, loving, God-fearing Christians… which is why across the street from Dinosaur World is a place called the Creation Evidence Museum.

The mission of the Creation Evidence Museum is to promote the literal, biblical accounts of the earth's creation, over and against the theory of evolution. People at that establishment believe the earth is closer to six thousand years old, not 4.5-billion. That is quite a difference.

Two extremes on either side of the road.

Which one is correct?

As a follower of Jesus in the Episcopal Church, I like to say that I comfortably drive down the road between those two establishments… I benefit from visiting each… and I believe God gives us minds to formulate our own decisions.

***

This morning, we have a reading from the Book of Genesis. People like to argue about the first eleven chapters of Genesis, especially the creation accounts.

Are they historical… or are they "merely" allegorical?

The tragic thing is this: we can waste time arguing about whether these chapters are historical or allegorical… and never arrive at the place of learning what the stories mean.

So, if you think the earth is six thousand years old and these stories are historical fact: great! The Episcopal Church Welcomes You.

If you believe the earth is 4.5-billion years old and these stories are allegorical: great! The Episcopal Church Welcomes You.

If you have never thought about this before and have not formed an opinion… or you could care less: great! The Episcopal Church Welcomes You.

So, what does this story mean?

God has created Adam and Eve, the first two humans. They are in the Garden of Eden. God has told Adam what fruit is permissible to eat in the garden, and what is not. We might infer that Adam has passed along this information to Eve… because all husbands and wives communicate perfectly.

So, here comes the serpent… an animal craftier than any other God fashioned… and notice that Scripture does not call the serpent The

Devil or Satan. It is simply a serpent. And the serpent asks Eve a question that we humans struggle with on a daily basis.

The question is this: Did God say?

Did God really say that?

Can God be trusted?

The serpent's position is that God CANNOT be trusted… God does NOT have humanity's best interests at heart… because, ultimately (according to the serpent) God may be hiding something from us, or maybe God is jealous of humanity.

How do we know this? The serpent tells Eve that if they eat the fruit God forbade, then humanity will become like God.

Do you hear that? That is the core of all sin… the notion that we can be like God… be God… that humanity can take the place of God.

Yes, theologians over the centuries have talked about how God became human in Jesus so humanity could become more divine. Humanity does have a role in co-creation … co-mission with God. But humanity can never take the place of God.

When we lose sight of this basic truth, just as Adam and Eve did… humanity suffers… and when humanity suffers, all of creation suffers.

Bad theology hurts ecology.

***

The counterpoint to the Genesis story about humanity's fall is found in today's Gospel lesson from Matthew.

The Spirit of God has led Jesus into the wilderness to be tempted by the devil. This is right after Jesus' baptism… when Jesus emerged from the water, and the voice of God the Father said: "This is my Son, the Beloved, with whom I am well pleased."

We must have the words of the Father in the backs of our minds as we hear the temptations placed before Jesus by the devil. Why? The devil sounds a lot like the serpent did when it spoke to Eve.

Notice that two of the temptations begin with the phrase: "If you are the son of God."

In other words, did God really say that?

"Yes, I know the Father just told you that you are his beloved, Jesus. But he didn't really mean that. You can get along in life just fine without the affirmation of God.

Go a different way. Go your own way. Go my way… bow down to me… and you will become popular, powerful, and prosperous."

***

Jesus was tempted by Satan in the same way Eve was tempted by the serpent.

But Jesus succeeds where Adam and Eve failed.

Jesus rebukes the devil… Jesus trusts that what God the Father has to say is life-giving and true… and then Jesus sets out on a ministry and mission to bring healing and wholeness to those he meets.

As we continue our Lenten journeys, may we trust more what God has to say.

Leave and Go

Words for March 12, 2017

This morning, as we continue our Lenten journey… a journey intended to move us away from sin and toward the God revealed to us in Jesus the Christ… instead of preaching what we might call a traditional sermon, I would like to tell a story.

The story is based on our reading from Genesis, which begins this way: "The Lord said to Abram, 'Go from your country and your kindred and your father's house to the land that I will show you.'"

According to Rabbi Jonathan Sacks, there are at least four other ways we can translate and understand God's command to Abram, who would become Abraham… and I would like to share these before getting to the story.

The first understanding of the Lord's command to Abraham would be: Journey FOR yourself. In other words, God tells Abram to travel for his own benefit and good… and at journey's end, God will make of Abram a great nation. Because, as of right now, Abram's life has come to a dead end.

The second understanding would be: Journey with yourself… which is to say, when Abram travels from place to place, he will extend his influence not over one land, but many.

A third understanding would be: Journey to yourself… meaning, Abram's journey… like our own Lenten and life journeys… such a journey takes us to the root of our souls.

A fourth understanding, according to Rabbi Sacks, would be: Journey by yourself… and that means, we can only become the people God calls us to be when we make a conscious decision to stop trying to be what others want us to be.

In light of these understandings, I would like to share some Jewish Midrash on Abram (Abraham) by Rabbi Robert Barr. Midrash is basically the elaboration… maybe improvisation… on a biblical story to bring out ethics, values, and more.

Here is what Rabbi Barr has to say about Abraham.[2] I invite you to meditate on this story as we move deeper into Lent.

***

Abraham had been in his father's idol shop many times. It was a family business. Terah, Abraham's father, inherited it from his father – who in turn had inherited it from his father before him. The designs for the idols sold there had been passed down from father to son for several generations. Though each added some new idols – the historic ones always seemed most in demand.

As it is in most family businesses, everyone had to help. There was much work to be done. To ensure a profit the family helped out when they could. Displays had to be set up, floors swept, records maintained, bills paid, and purchases delivered. For the most part, Abraham was responsible for delivering the idols. Terah would help Abraham load the idols upon a sturdy wooden cart and Abraham would pull it to the homes of those who had made recent purchases. Once at their home – the family would eagerly assist Abraham at removing the idol from the cart, carrying it to the special place they had selected, and erecting it with the kind of respect and devotion deserving of an idol.

Typically, Abraham would just shake his head and leave without uttering a word. He could not understand why people purchased idols – and he was dumbfounded by reverence which they demonstrated

---

[2] http://www.ourjewishcommunity.org/learn/midrashim-legends/abraham-and-the-idols/

toward the sculptures. Abraham knew how the idols were made – in fact he had helped. For him, the idols were simply stone…with eyes that could not see, ears that could not hear, mouths that could not speak, feet that could not move. But, still people would come to his father's shop – respectfully exploring the idols and choosing the one which most moved them.

Terah had always avoided leaving Abraham alone in the shop, because he knew of Abraham's disdain for idols and those who would purchase them. But, at times, Terah had no choice, as on this day when pressing business on the other side of town demanded his immediate attention. He left his son alone in the store.

A sense of dread came over Terah as he approached the store – he knew something was wrong. His steps quickened; nervously, Terah hurried to learn what had happened. As he entered his shop, the shop that once belonged to his father and his grandfather, he could not believe his eyes. It had been destroyed – displays were overturned, walls had holes in them, counters were on their sides, and all the idols were broken. Idols that had once been magnificent were now shattered pieces of stone. As Abraham stepped out from the back room – Terah asked, "Who did this horrible thing? Who hated me and my family so much they that would destroy our shop and thus our livelihood?"

Abraham hesitated before answering, "the largest idol did it – he took a hammer and destroyed the others before I could stop and destroy him." "Son, do you take me for a fool?" Terah shouted, "These are nothing but stone creations – you destroyed our shop – you destroyed our family's future!"

"If you know that they are but stone," asked Abraham, "why do you sell them – why do you allow people to believe that they are more than just sculpted rock?"

"It is not my place to take from people that which they hold dear," answered Terah, "I am here to give them what they ask for even though I myself do not believe that what they want is of value."

"That is a sham," declared Abraham, "that is deceitful and dishonest – I will not be a part of such a charade. I will leave this place – I will not return."

With that said, Abraham left his home, his family, and his past. He began his journey – vowing never to allow the idols of the past to be his security for the future.

Wolverines Do Not Share Things in Common with Buckeyes

Homily for March 19, 2017

There is a question that has been asked of me several times since moving here. It is this: "Fr. Curt (Curt, Pastor, Hey, You!), Michigan or Michigan State?" It is a fun, light-hearted question, to which I like to answer in a fun and light-hearted way. When given the option of Michigan or Michigan State, my response is "Yes."

This particular question is a conversation starter, an ice-breaker. But look at what kind of question it is. This is an "either/or" question designed to pin down somebody's allegiances. Once the questioner can label the person being questioned, then the questioner can choose how to relate to the person being questioned.

If the questioner gets a response deemed favorable, conversation will likely be amicable, and a deep friendship could develop.

If the person being questioned sports different colors than that of the questioner, the questioner then can safely cordon that person off in pre-conceived categories… and become dismissive of the person being questioned.

This is an extreme, cynical position, perhaps. But what is the default behavior of 21st Century Americans when ice-breaker questions move from sports to politics, or any contentious issue?

If I can label someone as "them" and not "us," then I can recuse myself from having to interact with them. And if I do interact with them, because they are "them" and we are "us," it is okay for "us" to demonize "them."

But might such questions say more about the questioner than they do about those being questioned?

And could it be that the "us versus them" distinction is inconsistent with the life of one who endeavors to follow Jesus?

***

In today's Gospel lesson, and because of today's Gospel lesson, we are introduced to three sets of persons who are slaves to labels... slaves and labels uncovered by Jesus' conversation with a Samaritan woman.

In no particular order, the first people enslaved to labels, strangely enough, are Jesus' disciples. They are astonished that Jesus is talking to a woman. Why would a man in first century Palestine be talking to a woman in public, since that woman is not his wife?

The disciples are so shocked that Jesus is talking to a woman that they do not have the courage to ask him why he is talking to her. It is not something people in those days did. People had become slaves to this custom. And, in a privileged sense, the male disciples could not see just how enslaved they were.

A second person enslaved by labels is the Samaritan woman herself. She is surprised that Jesus is talking to her because Jesus is Jewish, and she is a Samaritan. Our Gospel writer John points out, Samaritans do not share anything in common with Jews. John is being polite. Jews and Samaritans hated each other.

You see, Samaritans and Jews were distant cousins. Jews descended from the two southern tribes of Israel. Jesus, himself, comes from the blood line of the southern tribe of Judah.

Samaritans descended from the ten northern tribes of Israel and were not considered by Jews to be full-blooded Israelites. About eight centuries before the birth of Jesus, the king of Assyria had his troops invade Samaria. Many people from the ten northern tribes of Israel were taken into Assyrian captivity, and those Israelites who were left behind in Samaria inter-married with Assyrians. So, Jews in Jesus' day looked upon Samaritans with disdain. Samaritans were labeled as "them" and not "us."

The third group of people enslaved by labels because of this Gospel story... it is us. If we are honest, we have placed a label on somebody in this story. If we did not do it this morning with this particular person, then there is someone else we have encountered in our lives similar to the labeled person in this story… similar in how we have labeled them.

Did you hear about that Samaritan woman? She has had five husbands. Jesus says so. And that is not all! Jesus says the man she is with right now is not her husband.

Where do our minds go when we hear facts like that about a person, especially a woman?

She must be doing something wrong. This Samaritan woman… what is her name again? Oh, John doesn't tell us her name. But she must have had a name. Did that even cross our minds?

Over the centuries, theologians have made assumptions about this woman that are not in the text… and we have gone right along with those theologians. Some have said things like: if she has five husbands and is "shacked up" with another man right now, she must be a person of loose morals. Maybe she has earned a living through the world's oldest profession? But there is nothing in the text to support this claim, this label.

Maybe this woman's life has little to do with scandal, and more to do with tragedy. Has she been widowed? Did a husband or two simply walk out on her? Is she a strong woman who married insecure men?

We do not know her story. But we think we do.

When Jesus speaks to the Samaritan woman about her marriages, instead of assuming that he is telling her to repent… because Jesus does NOT tell her to repent… maybe Jesus is speaking into her pain, offering the relief that comes from simply talking with him.

Jesus removes the labels we apply… begins a conversation that neither the first disciples nor we would have started on our own… and when God in human flesh shows the woman respect and tells her that he knows who she is and what she has been going through, this Samaritan woman taps into the divine well-spring that satisfies the thirsty soul.

***

Several years ago, the cable sports channel ESPN ran a commercial in which a young couple… college-age… was sitting on a couch. At first, we can see only their faces. The couple is gazing into each other's eyes. The couple leans in to kiss each other… and as they kiss, the camera zooms out.

After a few seconds, we become startled by the labels affixed to these star-crossed lovers.

The girlfriend is wearing a University of Michigan sweatshirt, while the boyfriend is wearing an Ohio State sweatshirt: Michigan and Ohio State expressing true love for one another… even though Wolverines do not share things in common with Buckeyes.

Then words flash on the screen: "Without college sports, this wouldn't be disgusting."

***

May God give us the grace to promote LOVE over LABELS.

God and Blindness

Homily for March 26, 2017

When a child is presented for baptism in the Episcopal Church, the priest asks parents and godparents the following question: "Will you by your prayers and witness help this child to grow into the full stature of Christ?"

What does it mean to grow into the full stature of Christ Jesus?

It is a question appropriate for adult followers of Jesus, as well, since there are unforeseen events in life which present us with opportunities for growth. So, let us consider for a moment an element or two of what growth into the full stature of Jesus the Christ involves.

To be sure, there are things we must learn: the teachings of Jesus; the portrait Jesus paints of God the Father; God's dream for the world; and how a humanity empowered by the Holy Spirit works with God to make God's dream a reality.

It is important for us to learn through the lens of Jesus the overarching story of Holy Scripture, the message of the patriarchs and prophets… and the ways all of that informs how we view the death, resurrection, ascension, and eventual return of Christ.

For us to become mature followers of Jesus there are things we must learn.

By the same token, growth into the full stature of Christ involves a process of unlearning.

***

In today's Gospel lesson, Jesus and his disciples are out for a walk. On their journey, they encounter a man who was born blind.

The disciples ask Jesus: "Rabbi, who sinned, this man or his parents, that he was born blind?"

What did this man or his parents do wrong… what sin did they commit… that forced God to inflict this man with a difference, place the man at a disadvantage, and make him suffer for the rest of his life?

***

This question speaks volumes about how the disciples see God, and how their understanding of God influences the way they view and treat other people.

We can tell from their question that, at some level, they believe God's relationship with humanity is adversarial.

The disciples apparently have been living their lives in fear of making a mistake, in fear of sinning… because if they make a mistake, then God will retaliate… and everyone will see how God punishes them, and everyone will stand in judgment of them.

They believe in an angry god who is out to get us!

That is why, when the disciples see the man who was born blind, they immediately want Jesus to tell them who made God mad. If the disciples know who is to blame, they can be sure not to make the same mistake as the offender.

They do not want what they consider to be an abnormality to be contagious. They refuse to consider the possibility that difference comes about randomly in life. The disciples want to be in control, just as Adam and Eve sought control over their lives by eating the forbidden fruit.

It is the misguided notion that: if we can control God through our behavior, then we can make sure our lives are free from hardship and misery.

Whether we admit it or not, this is how we approach God from time-to-time. But this is a false understanding of God… which leads to, among other things, a humanity that is suspicious of one another.

This approach to God is alive and well in 21st Century America.

How often have we heard disciples of Jesus assign blame to a particular segment of humanity when a natural disaster strikes, or in the midst of a health crisis?

If we know whom to blame, we can keep our noses clean, and show God what good little children we are. But we cannot put God in our debt… which is why the American-made prosperity Gospel is a ruse.

Jesus says we need to unlearn this way of looking at God.

In today's Gospel lesson, Jesus is clear: neither the man born blind nor his parents sinned. They did nothing to incur God's wrath. And that means the man's blindness… his difference… was not caused by God. It is just one of those things.

So, instead of viewing the man and his parents with suspicion, followers of Jesus should look upon them in the same way God does: with compassion.

When Jesus' followers see life the same way God does, the door to healing opens.

***

This story from John's gospel begs the question: who is truly blind?

Yes, there is the man who was born physically blind.

But the disciples… as well as the religious elite of Jesus' day… were blind to the ways of God.

***

How might we today be blind to God's activity in Saginaw?

How might we misjudge people and events we initially deem wrong, sinful, or different?

And how might our recovery of sight… unlearning judgment and learning compassion… open the door for healing to take root in our community?

APRIL

A Columbarium for St. John's

Homily for April 2, 2017

I am not sure if anybody is keeping track of what has been taking place at St. John's during the new rector's first one hundred days. But if you are one of those with an eye for detail, today is day eighty-four.

And on this eighty-fourth day as your rector, I would like to spend a few moments speaking about a project that honors the legacy of St. John's… while, at the same time, keeps our eyes on the future God has for us.

In late January, I spoke about some of the hopes and projects for St. John's which many of you have communicated to me. One of the projects on our minds is the construction of a columbarium.

A columbarium, of course, is a place where the cremains of our loved ones are kept as we await the return of Christ. Some churches have columbaria outside a sanctuary or chapel, others have them inside. In either case, they are designed as holy places where we can remember, honor, and pray for our loved ones who are in God's direct presence.

This is something which has been in the discussion stage at St. John's for many years. Right now, please allow me to set us on a path to how we can, God willing, have a columbarium in place at St. John's by the Feast of All Saints on November 5th of this year.

Now, I will not stand here and guarantee this date. There are many factors to take into consideration. But I believe this should be our goal.

The first thing I would like to say about a columbarium project is that this is simply stage one. This is not something we will invest in in 2017 and never invest in again. We have faith that, over the decades and centuries, this is something future generations of St. John's will expand, enhance, and improve.

God's call on us at this moment is to be faithful in our day and take the initial step.

As we consider God's call, it is important to note that the presence of a columbarium at St. John's can help with the grief we experience when someone we love dies. A columbarium openly acknowledges death in a space where we hold out hope for resurrection.

While it is coincidence that today's gospel lesson from John speaks of Jesus bringing his dear friend Lazarus back to life, much of the passage gives us a window into the grief and anguish of Martha and Mary. They are devastated by the death of their brother, Lazarus… and they unleash their anger onto Jesus. We do that, too.

When someone close to us dies, we get angry; we get angry with God; we get angry with life, because life as we knew it in this world changes forever. There will always be a void in our souls created by the deaths of those we know and love.

And since that is the case, we must learn to deal with our grief in a healthy way. We must not place expectations on ourselves, or God, thinking there will ever come a time in this life when we no longer feel such a deep loss. It is perfectly normal and healthy for us to grieve at some level for the rest of our lives.

It is equally important, as followers in the way of Jesus, to understand that Christ stands alongside us in our grief; God cries with us.

What an image that is: the God who became human in Jesus shares our sorrows, absorbs our pain, and without diminishing our pain, offers to transform our pain into new life.

As Franciscan priest Richard Rohr likes to say: "If we don't allow God to transform our pain, we will transmit our pain to others."

Hurt people hurt people.

With the proper pastoral resources, a columbarium can be a tool to help us in our grief.

***

The vestry, staff members, and I are of a consensus that the first stage of the columbarium should be located in the chapel (up the ramp and to the left). Placement of a columbarium there allows for quiet reflection in a place where the Holy Eucharist is celebrated weekly. And, as a side note, I believe that placing the columbarium in the chapel will serve as a catalyst to beautify that space even more.

And let me be quick to point out that this is not to say that St. John's will never have a columbarium outside. We are speaking this morning only of a first step.

An individual or couple's investment in a columbarium niche is an investment not only in the space in which the cremains will be interred. It is an investment in the long-term viability of St. John's. It is a form of planned-giving that helps cover the cost of maintaining and enhancing the columbarium project. It makes the statement that St. John's endeavors to remain in Old Town Saginaw for a long time to come.

Initially, we are looking at a columbarium structure with about 48 niches. An estimated start-up cost, based on a few companies with whom we have spoken, will be in the neighborhood of $15,000. We already have about $5200 in the bank dedicated toward a columbarium project.

A companion niche, meaning there is enough space in a niche for the cremains of two people, can be reserved by members of St. John's for $1500, which is on the low end of what it costs to inter remains anywhere.

According to my rough math, to get this project moving as soon as possible, St. John's would need to have members invest in at least ten of the 48 niches.

While the vestry has some official documents that need to be finalized, we would need commitments from the St. John's faithful as soon as possible so that we could possibly have a columbarium in place by November 5, which is when the Church commemorates the Feast of All Saints this year.

Why All Saints? it is the feast on the Church Calendar which reminds us that through the death, resurrection, ascension, and eventual return of Christ, the living and the dead are still connected.

When we embrace the Feast of All Saints, typically held on the first day in November, as well as the Feast of All Faithful Departed on November 2, we make the audacious Christian claim that death does not have the final say.

Those "whom we love but see no longer" have not disappeared into oblivion.

Because of Jesus, our loved ones are being cared for by God. It is this hope, bolstered by the comfort of the Holy Spirit, which empowers us to carry on in our day.

A columbarium is not simply a nice piece of furniture. It is not a money-maker for St. John's.

A columbarium can help us in our grief; it can be a prophetic witness that honors our past; and it can move us forward along the path of God's future.

May God's will be done in this place.

Which Jesus Do We Choose?

Homily for April 9, 2017
Palm Sunday

Which Jesus do we choose?

I am not sure how many times over the years I had to read this passage from Matthew before I realized, before it was pointed out to me, that there are two men here named Jesus. There is Jesus of Nazareth whom we all know. And then there is a prisoner described by Matthew as being notorious of his day. His name was Jesus: Jesus Barabbas.

Pontius Pilate… the Roman Empire's top official in Judea… places Jesus of Nazareth and Jesus Barabbas side-by-side for us to compare and contrast, to choose or deny.

The events recorded by Matthew take place during the Jewish festival of the Passover. It is the time when the story of Moses and the Exodus of God's people from captivity in Egypt is at the forefront of everybody's mind.

As part of the many plagues inflicted on the Egyptians, God commanded Hebrew families to slaughter a lamb. The blood from the lamb was to be marked over the doorpost of each Hebrew family's home. When the angel of death visited, the angel of death passed-over the homes imprinted with, protected by, the lamb's blood.

And because Egyptian homes were without the blood of a lamb, the first-born male child in each Egyptian home died. That prompted Pharaoh to urge the Hebrews to leave Egypt… free to enter the wilderness… free to head for the Promised Land.

Each year, our Jewish sisters and brothers tell this story so that they will never forget how they were once oppressed… and how God liberated them.

***

On their minds in today's gospel lesson: who was God going to send to liberate them, not from the Egyptians, but the Romans?

One custom at that time was for the Roman government to release a Jewish prisoner during the festival of the Passover. Pontius Pilate gives the Jewish people a choice between two men named Jesus. And while each man has the same name, they could not be more different.

There is Jesus, whom we know as the Son of God the Father. And then there is Jesus Barabbas.

If we break down that name: "bar" means "son of" … "abba" means "father," as we learn elsewhere in the gospels.

Two men named Jesus: each the son of a particular father.

Each Jesus is, in his own way, a threat to the Roman government. But it is how each goes about his opposition to injustice that separates Jesus from Jesus.

Jesus Barabbas, again, is described by Matthew as "notorious" … by John as a "bandit" … by Mark and Luke as one involved in a "riot." It seems Jesus Barabbas is not opposed to using violence to create the kind of Palestine he wants for himself, his family, his friends, and his people.

Today, would we call Jesus Barabbas a terrorist?

***

Then there is Jesus of Nazareth, who endeavors to bring about God's kingdom on earth through love and peace. Jesus of Nazareth does not return the violence inflicted on him with violence. Jesus of Nazareth instead models a way to end humanity's cycle of violence.

Jesus of Nazareth becomes vulnerable on the Cross, freely subjecting himself to the torture of the Roman soldiers. In doing so, Jesus holds a mirror to humanity… and shows us just how cruel we can be to one another… and how, in the process of exacting violence on our own human race, we are guilty of violence against God.

Two different forms of resistance to oppression; each carries the name of Jesus.

But which Jesus does humanity consistently choose?

And I must point out here that we cannot simply blame the Jews for Jesus' death. Jesus was a Jew. What we need to understand this Holy Week is how all of humanity is complicit in the death of Jesus. No room for anti-Semitism or anti-Judaism.

With two thousand years of hindsight, it is easy for us to criticize the choice made with a herd mentality. The crowds demonstrating outside a government building chose the wrong Jesus.

They took to themselves the violent Jesus. That is the one for whom the people were screaming.

If we scream loudly enough, we will get the Jesus we want, right?

After all, why would anybody want a God whose strength is revealed in weakness?

***

Make no mistake. I am fully aware of the attraction to Jesus Barabbas… as well as my place in the crowd, from time-to-time.

And here is the thing: when I become aware of my knee-jerk temptation to choose Jesus Barabbas when life gets polarized… I can examine my motivations… and hold my motivations up to what is taught in this gospel passage… so that the Holy Spirit can nudge me in the way I should go, the way of Jesus of Nazareth.

How might our world transform if we were to defy the crowds… and allow a radically vulnerable God to be released into our midst?

It is difficult, slow work.

No instant gratification.

But it is the way God's kingdom becomes a reality on earth.

Which Jesus do we choose?

Uncomfortable

Homily for April 13, 2017
Maundy Thursday

Uncomfortable.

We find ourselves in the same room as the first disciples on the night before Jesus was lifted high on the Cross, around the same table, taking on the same posture before our Lord, and it is uncomfortable.

It can be uncomfortable anytime we have to discuss tonight's elephant in the middle of the room: death.

It is especially uncomfortable when a loved one has died or is near death.

While Jesus' passage through death helps us frame life, we can lose sight of this truth and spend much of our lives avoiding our own deaths. We distract ourselves in the name of living an active life. We ignore daily reminders of death by focusing on our health, regardless of whether the attention we give to our health is too much or too little.

When death pays a visit, our pain can be so great, our tears so ready to fall, that we choose not to talk about it, even with those we love, those who could help us most through our grief.

It can be uncomfortable.

***

The words on the Church calendar can bring discomfort.

Maundy Thursday.

Thursday is not so bad. But Maundy? When some hear that word for the first time, they think they hear Monday: the second-day of the Christian week, the first-day of the work week for many.

But it is not Monday. It is M-A-U-N-D-Y, from the Latin for mandate.

Jesus gives his first and current disciples a new mandate, a new commandment to love one another. We are to love one another in the same way Jesus loves us. And it is through this love for one another that everyone will know we follow Jesus.

That is easier said than done.

The Christian life is easier said than done.

The Christian life is not always comfortable.

***

Tonight, we offer the experience of foot-washing, something we may fear more than death.

No one here should feel compelled to participate in this ritual. I am not here to make you uncomfortable. But we cannot ignore the discomfort.

It is not inherently wrong for us to be anxious about having our feet washed by another. Simon Peter, at first, refused to allow Jesus to wash his feet.

But why? Could Peter's discomfort be ours?

***

It was customary in Jesus' day for servants to wash the feet of their master. Technically, since Jesus was the master, Peter was to serve Jesus, right? That is how things work in corporate America: Jesus is the senior partner, Peter a junior partner, therefore Peter would be the one washing Jesus' feet.

But the Jesus Movement does not (should not) look like 21st Century Western Capitalism.

The God of the Bible is not a brass ring to be obtained through upward mobility.

Think of Jacob and Esau from the Book of Genesis.

These brothers jockeyed for position in the womb of their mother Rebekah.

Jacob, whose name means "heel-grabber" or "deceiver," tugged at the feet of his older twin Esau from birth to adulthood.

Their father, Isaac, loved Esau more than Jacob. So, Jacob had to live a life of deception to be on the receiving end of his father's love.

Jacob did this because he recognized there were limits to his father Isaac's so-called love.

***

When something we need is in short supply, especially love, we resort to deception.

In the name of controlling our own destiny in times of scarcity, we become someone other than the person God has created us to be.

We are desperate.

When we are desperate, we compete.

When we compete, life is a zero-sum-game.

For me to win, you must lose. I must be in control.

Everybody must die… except for me.

For Jacob to win, Esau and everybody else who came across Jacob's path would have to lose.

But Jacob eventually realized that the zero-sum-game – a kind of B.C. March Madness – is not the way of God.

***

Tonight, Jesus reinforces this lesson with our feet.

For us to love one another in such a way that the world takes notice, we must first accept the love God becomes for us in Jesus… die to the notion of placing limits on love… and embody God's love for humanity.

God's love is not scarce.

God's love has no limits.

God's love does not divide the world into "winners and losers," "loved and unloved."

With God, all are loved.

***

To encounter this truth, we must become vulnerable.

It is vulnerability that challenges the hubris which says Jesus does not need to wash my feet.

It is vulnerability that brings us to the sobering reality that in life and death we are not in control.

It is vulnerability that reminds us it is the God we know in Christ Jesus who is in control of our life and our death.

And since that is the case, we are invited to place our lives in the hands of the one who IS in control… trust him with our life and death… receive love and comfort from the community that bears his name…. and, in turn, offer God's love and comfort to others.

Jesus says:

Let me wash your feet.

Let me love and comfort you.

Love one another, just as I love you.

What Do We Do with the Body of Christ?

Homily for April 14, 2017
Good Friday

What do we do with the Body of Christ?

Let us consider for a moment some of the people who interact with Jesus as he is arrested, tortured, and dies.

As we read through this passage, we see women and men of different backgrounds: cultural, racial, national, social, political, and religious. What do they do with Jesus? How might we see ourselves in them?

***

There is Judas Iscariot, the disciple who betrayed Jesus. Judas hands over the Body of Christ to a lynch mob with lanterns, torches, and weapons. Was Judas hoping his actions would cause Jesus to bring about God's kingdom with a display of force?

How might we betray the Body of Christ to bring about a world we desire, through methods other than God's?

***

Then there is the religious establishment and its police force. Their task was to bind and detain the Body of Christ. When we deem someone as a threat, that is what we do to them. We restrict movement of, and access to.

It is interesting to me that Jesus is the one who is detained, after Simon Peter took a weapon and cut off the ear of the high priest's slave. Jesus ordered Peter to drop his weapon. Jesus posed no physical threat to the soldiers, the high priest's slave, or anyone else. In Luke's gospel, we are told that Jesus touched the slave's ear and healed it.

Peter is not the one taken into custody. Jesus is.

How is it that a man of peace poses a greater threat than a man with a weapon?

How often are we so threatened by the Body of Christ that we bind and detain him? How might we place God in a box?

***

Simon Peter is a roller coaster of emotions. At one moment, he is ready to fight to the death for Jesus. But when Jesus tells him that violence is not the answer, Peter must have set out on a journey of introspection.

Why did Jesus not want me to be so zealous for him in that moment?

Why would I hurt others to protect the Body of Christ?

Could Peter have thought: do I really understand what it means to follow Jesus?

When recognized as one who was part of Jesus' group, Peter denies any association with the Body of Christ.

Has Peter's certainty about Jesus as the Son of the living God cast doubt on what such a confession might mean?

How might our distorted certainties about the ways of God actually deny the Body of Christ?

And might a distorted certainty do as much violence to the Body of Christ as that of the goons working on behalf of the religious establishment?

***

Maybe we are like Pontius Pilate. Here is a man who should have listened to his wife.

In Matthew's gospel, we are told that the wife of Pontius Pilate begged her husband to avoid the Body of Christ.

She said: "Have nothing to do with that innocent man, for today I have suffered a great deal because of a dream about him." (Matthew 27:19)

Pilate stands in a long line of men who should have listened to their spouses. But he also acts in a way that resonates with each and every one of us in this room.

There are situations in life that we could handle more easily if we had never come face-to-face with the Body of Christ.

I think Pilate knew deep down that Jesus was innocent. But external pressure groups caused Pilate to avoid what he sensed internally.

Did this politician violate his conscience to appease a special interest group?

How do we **side-step** the Body of Christ in our own day?

***

Fortunately, there is some good news in this passage.

We are told of the women who stayed near Jesus as his death approached. Mary, the mother of Jesus. His mother's sister, Mary the wife of Clopas [Cleopas]. And Mary Magdalene.

Lots of Marys attended to the Body of Christ.

With their attendance at the foot of the Cross… instead of betraying like Judas, acting out and denying like Peter, or side-stepping like Pilate… these women experienced the paradox of the Christian faith.

When standing near Jesus as he approached death, the women were attended to by the Body of Christ.

In the midst of life's difficulties, can we attend to the Body of Christ and remember that the tomb will be empty?

***

And, yes, there are men in this story with redeeming qualities: Joseph of Arimathea and Nicodemus.

This is the first time in John's gospel that we are introduced to Joseph of Arimathea. He is described as a "secret" disciple of Jesus.

Here is a man whose life "following Jesus by stealth" was dictated by fear, fear of being ostracized if not killed by the religious authorities… fear of losing his place in the community… fear of leaving behind the life he had known for the life he could see with Jesus.

But now that Jesus has been killed, it seems Joseph of Arimathea no longer has time for fear to guide his life. He is a secret follower of Jesus no more as he approaches Pontius Pilate, a public official, to claim the Body of Christ.

When Joseph claims the Body of Christ, he proclaims his faith in Jesus.

***

While we meet Joseph for the first time, we meet Nicodemus for the third time in John's gospel.

Nicodemus first came to Jesus under the cover of darkness, knowing there was something different about Jesus. But Nicodemus, like Joseph of Arimathea, is limited by fear.

At one point, as the religious authorities debated what to do with Jesus, Nicodemus raised his voice in a tempered defense of Jesus. And the authorities began to wonder if Nicodemus desired to become a follower of Jesus.

In today's gospel lesson, told maybe to show the progression of this man's walk with Jesus, we find that Nicodemus shows up to dignify the Body of Christ.

Nicodemus has expensive perfumes to anoint the body of Christ as he and others wrap the Lord's body in a proper cloth as part of the Jewish burial custom.

There are times when dignifying a loved one's death helps to better understand their life and our place in it.

How might we give dignity to the Body of Christ?

***

As we reflect on Jesus' death… we see in the biblical characters traits that reside in us.

When relating to the Body of Christ, at times we betray, bind, deny, and avoid.

When we become aware of these postures, we can then attend and dignify.

What do we do with the Body of Christ?

Progression

Homily for April 15, 2017
Easter Vigil – Genesis 22:1-18

God said to Abraham: "Take your son, your only son Isaac, whom you love, and go to the land of Moriah, and offer him there as a burnt offering on one of the mountains that I shall show you."

What a horrific story this is, or at first seems to be.

What do we make of the idea that the God we have come to know as Love once commanded a faithful follower to kill his own son? It is almost as bad as thinking that one human's suffering could be the direct result of a wager God placed with the Devil, the premise upon which the book of Job is built.

Some theologians claim this story, known as the Akedah, is designed to show Abraham that his future rests not in his progeny, but through faith in God. And while that sentiment is true on some level, there must be more to this story.

What if Abraham's near sacrifice of his son Isaac represents a progression: a progression of who Abraham thinks God is, a progression of how Abraham is to relate to this God, and a progression of how humanity thinks of and relates with the God of not only Abraham, but with the God of Isaac?

After all, the Bible is a library full of progressions. The book of Genesis, itself, moves us through the progressions of sibling rivalries: Cain and Abel, Isaac and Ishmael, Jacob and Esau, Joseph and his brothers, not to mention Rachel and Leah. Along the way, we eavesdrop on family disputes which end with murder on one extreme, varying degrees of tolerance in the middle, and almost full reconciliation at the end of Genesis. There is progression.

The book of Exodus speaks of the progression of God's people, as well. Moses moves from the slave quarters, to the palace, to the desert, back to the palace on behalf of the slaves. We know the identity of Moses the entire time. But Moses does not.

He thinks he is Egyptian royalty, learns he is a Hebrew slave, and when the life he thought he knew comes crashing down, Moses discovers he is a chosen one of God. He belonged not in the palace but in the slave quarters and was called on to move God's people from slavery to freedom, from darkness to light. There is progression.

Abraham was called by God to a path of progression, to leave his country and his kindred, and go to the place God would show him. God promised to make of Abraham a great nation. God would bless him and make Abraham's name great. God would bless those who blessed Abraham, and curse those who did not.

It was a progression from his father Terah's idolatry to his own understanding of the one, true God.

For the longest time, Abraham and his wife Sarah could not have children… which made others look down on them.

So, when God promised this infertile couple a child, their level of disbelief, rooted in a painful history, led to Sarah offering her Egyptian slave-girl Hagar to Abraham.

From that union came Ishmael. And while Ishmael would be blessed by God in a particular way, God's promise to Abraham would be fulfilled through his and Sarah's son, Isaac.

Given all that took place before Isaac's birth, why would God command Abraham to kill Isaac?

Can God not be trusted to keep promises?

Has Abraham regressed to a point in his life where he misunderstands God and, thus, God's command?

Reading this story on a surface level, this is not the kind of God in whom I want to believe. Why would I want to worship a god that commands me to eliminate the good around me which I hold dear? I would not. And because the answer seems obvious, I have to dig a bit deeper.

What if, instead, this story says more about me than it does about God? Since it is clear to me that I would not worship a god that would call on me to sacrifice my children for the sake of that god, and because many stories in the bible are used as literary devices to open our hearts and minds, maybe I should start looking to see if the traits attributed to God and Abraham in this story, which I detest, somehow exist in me.

What if I actually "sacrifice" others in my attempts to get closer to God and appear holy to those from whom I seek validation?

What if I treat the people God has placed in my life as means to an end?

What if I use my religion for selfish purposes and not for the benefit of others?

Maybe one point of this story is to have us ask the question: is my devotion to God, my religion, outward focused, a religion that moves the human experiment from darkness to light?

Or is my devotion to God, my religion, self-centered... focused only on me... a bogus religion that punches a one-way ticket to darkness?

When we ask ourselves such questions, we open the door for a progression to take place in our lives. When we dig beneath the surface of this troubling story, and not avoid it, our gaze can shift from Abraham's unquestioning, self-serving obedience to God... and focus on Isaac's inquisitive, self-giving obedience to both his father and to God.

***

When Abraham began the journey of religious devotion, his son, Isaac, asked him: "Where is the lamb for the burnt offering?"

Abraham's response to Isaac: "God himself will provide the lamb."

I am not sure if Abraham fully understands the answer he gives Isaac. But Isaac does. And I am glad for Isaac, since he does not come off looking that great as the father of Jacob and Esau.

Because Isaac trusts in the proclamation that God himself would provide a lamb for a burnt offering, or in Greek "holocaust," Isaac could then offer himself in service to his father and to God.

Isaac could be vulnerable and willingly risk his own life, trusting that God would provide. And because God provided Christ Jesus as the ultimate lamb who would bridge the gap between God and humanity, we know that it is through the religious act of Christ-like self-giving that humanity can move from darkness to light.

Devotion to the God we know in Christ Jesus comes not through self-serving, but through self-giving.

The path to God and a mature humanity comes not from a journey to the highest mountain.

The path to God and humanity's salvation passes through an Empty Tomb, because it is in the Empty Tomb where we learn that God keeps God's promises.

Michigan Cold

Homily for April 16, 2017
Easter Day – John 20:1-18

Alleluia! Christ is Risen!
The Lord is Risen Indeed! Alleluia!

If you would indulge me, I would like to offer a brief word of thanksgiving as we begin this message.

I have had the privilege of serving some faithful, Spirit-filled congregations in the Episcopal Church in almost 16 years of ordination. Margaret, Karina, Cade, and I could not be more thrilled to be here with you as we journey together. The St. John's community is fantastic. And we could not be more excited about what God has in store.

Having said that, if you had told me when I was ordained deacon in 2001 that I would one day be rector of a church in Michigan, I am not sure I would have believed you. I was born in Virginia, grew up in North Carolina and Illinois (southern Illinois), attended college and lived much of my adult life in Texas, went to seminary in Tennessee, and spent short amounts of time in California and New Mexico.

While each of those states has periods of cold, it is not Michigan cold. And I am told this year was a mild Michigan winter. And, so, why did God have the Normans move to mid-Michigan in the dead of winter?

People think we are nuts. I can tell by their questions:

Why did you move from Texas to Michigan in December?
Job.

Do you have family in Michigan?

No.

Have you ever been to Michigan before?
No.

It is at that point when people begin to back away from us.

But there is one thing we have learned right away about living in Michigan cold. You see, most other places we have lived would totally shut down schools and businesses with trace amounts of snow or ice. Just the tiniest bit of frozen precipitation, along with persistent gray skies, cause people to lock themselves inside their homes, turn up the heater, and go back to sleep under the covers. In those places, people have little experience of living in extended cold with longer, darker days. Who can blame them for wanting to hibernate when the cold visits?

But here, I have learned that Michiganders know how to navigate the cold. Yes, there is enough wisdom to know when it is time to hunker down in place. But there is also a confidence to live in the midst of cold. A few inches of snow do not deter people from getting out and doing what needs to be done. And when someone leaves the perceived safety of a warm home, they discover that life can actually be lived in the cold. While every single bank teller and grocery store clerk has told me they have plans to move to Florida, there is warmth in the midst of cold.

***

One morning about two thousand years ago, according to our gospel writer and patron Saint John, it was dark. Actual weather aside, the forecast that day for followers of Jesus was cold and gray. Their beloved friend had been executed the Friday before; Jesus was dead. The source of their warmth had been extinguished.

Despite that, Mary Magdalene, one of the women who stood at the foot of the Cross while Jesus freely offered his life, ventured out into the cold. In her grief, she must have been restless, unable to sleep, unable to find contentment in her retreat from the bitter climate.

In her journey through darkness, Mary Magdalene stumbled upon a gray area.

Jesus' body was not in the grave. The large stone covering the cave-tomb had been rolled away.

Mary Magdalene hurried back to the other disciples and told them what she had seen, and what she had not seen. Peter and John raced to the Empty Tomb to investigate. And because it seems they did not fully understand the meaning of an Empty Tomb, it is a bit much to wrap our heads around, those disciples went back home. They retreated from the cold and gray, even though they might have caught a small glimpse of the sun coming up over the horizon.

For whatever reason, Mary Magdalene's intuition told her that she could navigate the cold and gray. She was not afraid to cry at the deathbed, and she is not afraid to cry in the cemetery. And she is confident in the search for her Lord, even when she does not immediately recognize someone she already knows, someone who already knows her.

***

"Woman, why are you weeping?"
"They have taken away my Lord, and I do not know where they have laid him."

Woman, why are you weeping? For whom are you looking?

***

When it gets cold, and we venture out into the dark and are confronted with gray, whom do we look for? Where do we seek warmth, peace, wholeness, contentment?

Following the death of Jesus, many of his closest disciples retreated from the cold and gray. In their minds, even though Jesus had taught them otherwise, many disciples had fallen victim on that first Easter morning to the notion that death had the final word.

They thought eternal warmth had given way to extended cold.

They thought there was nothing worthwhile to experience at the place of death. So, they pulled back from life.

Mary Magdalene somehow knew differently.

Yes, she grieved her Lord's death.

But while at first, she did not recognize the new life standing right in front of her, Mary Magdalene persisted through the cold and gray.

She could not find whom she was looking for until she kept searching for whom she was looking for.

And when her focus shifted from "cold and gray" to "warmth and sunshine," Mary Magdalene turned from the need to cling to nostalgia. When the Risen Christ called her by name, Mary Magdalene flung open her arms, ready to receive something new from God.

***

This morning, if your heart is burdened with sadness… if you are not exactly sure why you have ended up here in the midst of your cold and gray… if you do not feel like you can see what you think others are seeing… if your intuition is calling on you to persist where others turn back… I have good news for you.

Keep searching… Christ will speak to you… and you will be prepared to receive new life from God.

Alleluia! Christ is Risen!
The Lord is Risen Indeed! Alleluia!

Going, Going, Gone

Homily for April 23, 2017
The Second Sunday of Easter

Every year on this day, the Second Sunday of Easter, the Church around the world tells the story of the disciple Thomas. It has become popular to refer to this follower of Jesus as Doubting Thomas, and that moniker has made its way into common usage.

Thomas is called “doubting” because he was absent when Christ was raised from the dead and appeared to the ten disciples.

(Remember, Judas has caved in to his despair by this point.)

So, when the ten and (likely) others in the group try to tell Thomas they had seen the Lord, he does not buy it.

In fact, there are some theologians who say the adjective “doubting” may not (or should not) apply to Thomas. One could interpret the Greek word in such a way that Thomas simply does not believe. But a “disbelieving” Thomas is not as poetic as a “doubting” Thomas.

What I wonder is: Where did Thomas go?

Just reading on the surface, the word “go” seems to be associated with Thomas each time he speaks in John’s gospel.

In the eleventh chapter, when Jesus says he is going to Bethany because his friend Lazarus has died, Thomas says: “Let us also go, that we may die with him.” (John 11:16)

In the fourteenth chapter, when Jesus speaks of his eventual death, resurrection, and ascension, Thomas says: “Lord, we do not know where you are going. How can we know the way?" (John 14:5) Jesus then says to Thomas: "I am the way, and the truth, and the life."

In John's gospel, Thomas was going, going, gone.

But where did Thomas go?

The more I read about Thomas, the more I think he struggles with the concept that Resurrection follows death.

And not just the literal Resurrection of Jesus following his death… because if Jesus is not literally raised from the dead, we can find other things to do on a Sunday morning… but Resurrection in the sense that good can be brought out of bad, joy can overcome despair, renewal can rise from decay.

I sometimes think Thomas disappeared from the pages of Scripture because the world was spinning so fast he had to get off for a moment. After all, Jesus had died. Losing someone close to us is painful. People grieve in different ways. Some need to be around others to process pain and loss. Others, like me, have to step into the shadows.

Leave me alone. Let me do what I have to do in private. I will resurface.

When Thomas resurfaces, he goes back to the people he had been around for the previous three years. Friendly faces, familiar voices, tender hearts who would cry with him.

But when Thomas rejoined the group, those disciples of Jesus were not crying tears of sadness… if they were crying, they were shedding tears of joy.

They tell Thomas: "We have seen the Lord."

Death is overcome.

The very thing we thought could defeat us is not such an obstacle after all.

But Thomas would not believe. The words of his friends were only that: words. Thomas needed more than head knowledge of the Lord's Resurrection. Thomas needed to touch the Risen Jesus himself before he could move his heart past "Christ has died" to "Christ is Risen."

And because Thomas needed more, the Risen Christ delivered. And I believe we have those ten other disciples to thank for this.

You see, we have no record of Peter and the others chastising Thomas for being absent when the Risen Christ first showed up. Thomas is not ostracized for his disbelief. Thomas is not kicked out of the inner-circle because he is not fully on board.

As far as I can tell, the other disciples that first Easter week must have loved Thomas, cared for him, listened to him, and consoled him, all the while gently telling him: yes, Jesus has been raised from the dead.

Yes, Resurrection follows death.

Yes, good can be found in the midst of the bad.

Yes, joy can overcome despair.

Yes, renewal can rise from decay.

And because those ten disciples kept Thomas close to them in his doubt or outright disbelief, it was not long before Thomas could see the Risen Christ and declare: "My Lord and my God!"

***

A few weeks ago, I read something in our local newspaper that highlighted symptoms of despair and decay in the City of Saginaw. What I learned bothered me to the point that I reached out to some folks I have met recently, and they graciously set up a meeting.

At that meeting… and I am fully aware that I am being vague here… but at that meeting, I listened to people who are on (for lack of a better term) the "front lines" in our community.

As I listened to them, I reflected on conversations I have had with many of you about the City of Saginaw: the city's booming population when General Motors was rising high… the decline when jobs once performed by people were taken over by automation… the blight which followed flight.

Going, going, gone.

As I was driving back to St. John's after that meeting, I was wondering what my role in Saginaw should be as a parish priest… and I was wondering what the role of St. John's should be, as people who pray in Old Town.

I wonder this because Saginaw's "minds of doubt" need to give way to "hearts of hope" … in fact, I believe that change is happening… and for that change to be good and lasting, St. John's needs to be St. John's.

We are Easter people who proclaim:

Christ has died! Christ is Risen! Christ will come again!

Yes, there is death, despair, and decay around us.

But because we know Christ has been raised from the dead… because we are ambassadors of hope… it is our God-given mission to be Easter people in Saginaw! Not just with words… but through incarnation… through our presence and touch.

As we prayerfully and thoughtfully engage our community outside these walls, may we boldly proclaim our Easter message:

Yes, resurrection follows death.

Yes, good can be discovered in the midst of bad.

Yes, joy can overcome despair.

Yes, renewal can rise from decay.

Alleluia! Christ is Risen! The Lord is Risen Indeed! Alleluia!

Journey to Emmaus

Homily for April 30, 2017

Last week, we reflected on Thomas, the disciple of Jesus who was not present with the others when the Risen Christ appeared to them. And we asked the question: Where did Thomas go?

This morning, we are immersed in what I consider to be a mysterious Gospel passage from St. Luke the Evangelist which could leave us with as many questions as answers. And as we walk beside these two followers of Jesus, as well as the Risen Christ, one question we might ask is: Who are they?

Luke identifies one of the disciples: Cleopas. The other is not named, which leads to some fun speculation. There are those in theological circles who say Cleopas might actually be Clopas. We remember Clopas from John's Gospel. His wife, Mary… whose sister was Mary the mother of Jesus… Mary the wife of Clopas was present with Jesus' mother and Mary Magdalene at the foot of the Cross, attentive to Jesus as he died.

Because Clopas (or Cleopas) is a man… and because biblical writers sometimes leave out the names of women… although in Luke's case such an omission may be out of deference, given the women's insistence on an empty tomb and conversations with angels… it could very well be that these two disciples on the road to Emmaus are Jesus' aunt and uncle.

Another question we can ask is: Where are Cleopas and his companion going?

Luke tells us it is Easter day in this passage, and these two are on their way to Emmaus, a village about seven miles from Jerusalem. Biblical archaeologists do not agree on the location of Emmaus. There are multiple sites under consideration.

The name Emmaus means something like "hot springs." it is a place where people of Jesus' day might have gone for refreshment, a first-century day spa. Some even define Emmaus as being a place of our "earnest longing" … the location of our "deepest desire."

As appealing as that spiritual definition might be, I have not yet found anything to indicate this was an original meaning of Emmaus. But I reserve the right to change my mind, if I am presented with new evidence.

***

One question the Risen Christ asks in this passage is: What are you talking about?

As we are introduced to Cleopas and his companion, we are told they are discussing the events of what we now call Holy Week: which of course would include Jesus' entry into Jerusalem, the Last Supper, Jesus' betrayal and arrest, his trial, death by crucifixion, as well as the empty tomb discovered by some women who followed Jesus.

Cleopas and his companion are trying to make sense out of what happened to Jesus, and likely wondering what will become of them and the ministry Jesus started.

This is NOT an uplifting discussion. We are told that they look sad. Their hope for the future has been dashed.

While they walked and talked, the Risen Christ joins them. But they do not recognize him right away.

Why not?

In the midst of grief like that of Cleopas and his companion, how difficult is it for us to experience Resurrection?

Might the proclamation of Resurrection ring hollow when we hurt?

As the Risen Christ approaches these two in their grief, Jesus wants to know what they are discussing. Cleopas is taken aback: "Are you the only stranger in Jerusalem who does not know the things that have taken place there in these days?"

Ironically, it appears that Jesus is the only one in Jerusalem who knows what has taken place. And the Risen Christ does not keep that information to himself.

As this group continues their journey along the road to Emmaus… to that place of refreshment, maybe to the location of earnest longing… Jesus explains the Scriptures to them… Jesus explains Life to them… reminding them of things he had once taught them, (to which they were reluctant to fully give their hearts.)

When Cleopas and his companion arrive at their destination, the Risen Christ… still not recognized by them… appears as if he wants to continue walking and talking. And this raises additional questions in my mind:

Did the Risen Christ have more to teach them?

Is there more we can learn from the Risen Christ when we understand that religion… while needing fixed points… is not always about arriving at a static location?

Cleopas and his companion beg their unknown friend to stay with them where they are now. The Risen Christ does just that. He communes with them at table, blesses the bread, breaks it, and shares it with them like he had done so many times before.

It is through these actions that Cleopas and his companion see the Risen Christ for who he is.

When we journey on a path to learn the Scriptures and share Holy Communion, we put ourselves in a place to see the Risen Christ for who he is… and when we experience Christ in our midst, there is Emmaus; there is refreshment, a satisfaction of our earnest longing.

Have biblical archaeologists not found Emmaus because they are looking without, and not within?

***

As the Risen Christ vanishes from this passage, so does the sadness of these disciples. Their grief has been transformed into hope. Their hearts are full. And because their joy cannot be contained, these two venture into the darkness of night to proclaim the message we are entrusted with today:

Alleluia! Christ is Risen!
The Lord is Risen Indeed! Alleluia!

MAY

Jésus est le Bon Berger

Homily for May 7, 2017

I am always intrigued by some of the expectations we have of God, the Church, and Clergy.

A long time ago in a parish far away, I was sitting in the waiting room of a doctor's office. As I watched the door that led to and from the examination rooms, out came a woman who could best be described as a nominal member of the church where then I was rector. While a perfectly wonderful person, she darkened the doors of the church less often than those who show up only on Christmas and Easter, two happy days on the Church calendar.

Before she could leave the doctor's office, she saw me sitting among other soon-to-be patients. I was all dressed in black with a full, white clerical collar surrounding my neck… because that is apparently how I dress to go see the doctor. This woman stopped dead in her tracks. Her jaw dropped to the floor. But she picked it up enough to look at me square in the eye and say in a surprised voice:

"Oh, I guess priests get sick, too." Yes, priests get sick, too. What was she expecting?

Then there is a common expectation we sometimes place on God: it is the mindset that says if I think, say, and/or do the right thing, God will reward me, and nothing will ever go wrong in my life. I will get a raise at work. I will find that choice parking spot at Target. I will never have a severe illness. Life should always be butterflies and unicorns.

People who approach God, expecting transaction and not transformation, are greatly disappointed when they in fact do the right things, but life still does not go their way.

I mention this because Reverend Pam and I sat down recently and held an impromptu, healthy session of lament. We talked with one another about some of the difficulties each of us has had in the past, as well as a few of the current challenges we face. Nothing tabloid worthy. It is just life.

As we talked, Pam (the French professor and world traveler), articulated a French expression:

"La vie n'est pas un long fleuve tranquille."

That translates into English: Life is not a long, tranquil river.

It does not take much time in reflection to see the turbulence in life created by relational stress, finances, sickness, and more. The river of life can have an undertow, send us over rocky rapids, and flood our shores. There are times when life is too much to take in, and we wonder if there is anything more coming our way. Life is not a long, tranquil river.

In times of disquiet we question the meaning of life, maybe the existence of God, or at least the existence of a God who cares for and interacts with humanity. And if the God I was hoping for, the God I was expecting, does not exist, why should I bother going to church on Sunday?

I do not mean to sound flippant or diminish anyone's pain, but might we need to adjust our expectations of God, Christianity, and the Church?

You see, it is precisely in moments of struggle and grief when we should deepen our relationship with the Church, open the Scriptures, and receive the Body and Blood of Christ.

The Christian Church does not exist on this side of heaven to lead people into a carefree life.

Instead, our Eucharistic worship is the nourishment we need to wrestle with, and process, the axiom: Life is not a long, tranquil river.

***

We just recited the 23rd Psalm. It is a popular one, recited often at funerals, many times in the language of the King James Bible. It speaks of the Lord as a shepherd guiding us by still waters, leading us through the valley of the shadow of death.

That line in which the psalmist talks about the Lord as our shepherd leading us beside the still waters… the word used in the French translation of the 23rd Psalm is tranquil, the same word we hear in the French expression about life.

So, on one hand we acknowledge that life is not a long, tranquil river. And on other hand, we hear the promise of God.

In the midst of the turbulence of life… poetically depicted as the valley of the shadow of death… God shepherds us to tranquil waters.

The goal of the Christian life is eternal union with God, in Christ Jesus, through the power and presence of the Holy Spirit. Too often, we think of that goal as something which happens only after we die from this life; it can take on a fairy tale like quality. When it does, we fail to consider the possibility of God breaking into our lives now so that we can experience tranquil waters in the midst of life's turbulence.

Given all the hardship we see in our own lives and those of others, I understand the desire to disengage.

But when life becomes too much to bear, is there somewhere we can turn for peace? Is there someone to whom we can turn to help us navigate the river of life? Is there a path to still, quiet, tranquil waters in the midst of death's shadows?

Not long after Pam shared with me the French expression that "life is not a long, tranquil river" … she discovered that was only half of the expression.

The full expression is: LA VIE N'EST PAS UN LONG FLEUVE TRANQUILLE, MAIS ELLE OFFRE QUELQUES ÎLES DE TENDRESSE.

Life is not a long, tranquil river, but it offers a few islands of tenderness.

The God who comes to us in Christ Jesus is the one who shepherds us to life's islands of tenderness. This happens when we take our place in the Body of Christ, listen for Jesus to call each of us by name, and allow him to guide us to abundant life.

Alleluia! Christ is Risen!
The Lord is Risen Indeed! Alleluia!

Forgiveness

Homily for May 14, 2017

Happy Mother's Day to all who are mothers, as well as those who are motherly. While this is a greeting card holiday, and not on the Church calendar, we cannot deny the impact this day has on our culture, in good ways… and in some cases difficult.

For those of us on social media, we see tributes in both word and picture from persons thanking their mother for helping to shape their lives. And when such posts are memorial in nature, some convey how they wish their mother were still alive, so they can tell their mother just how much of an impact she had.

We are also in the liturgical season of graduation: caps, gowns, and diplomas. Social media posts show pictures of graduates with teachers who have influenced these students in their academic careers. In some cases, the teachers are surprised with the impact they had on the students.

***

In today's reading from Acts of the Apostles, St. Luke the Evangelist introduces us to a follower of the Risen Christ named Stephen. Stephen is described as "… a man full of faith and the Holy Spirit" (Acts 6:5), also as being "full of grace and power, (who) did great wonders and signs among the people." (Acts 6:8)

We learn in Acts 6 that as the number of the Risen Christ's followers was increasing, there was disagreement. It seems the Greek-speaking widows following in the Way of Jesus were not getting a fair share of the daily food distribution. The Apostles then appointed Stephen and six others to attend to the needs of the entire community.

The Church considers these seven to be the first deacons.

Stephen is a powerful preacher. The religious elite are so threatened by what Stephen says about Jesus that they drum up false charges of blasphemy. Stephen is put before a religious council, and when Stephen shows how the God of Abraham, Isaac, and Jacob, the God of Moses brings salvation of the cosmos through Jesus of Nazareth, that is heresy to the religious establishment.

Stephen is sentenced to capital punishment; death by stoning.

As Stephen approaches his own death, we see his resolve as a follower of the Risen Christ.

Stephen (again) is filled with the Holy Spirit and sees Jesus standing at the right hand of God the Father.

Stephen has faith that the Resurrection of Christ opens the door to eternal life with God.

This Resurrection faith gives Stephen confidence to place his current situation in its proper perspective, and thus speak God's truth in the here and now.

With Resurrection faith, Stephen is able to absorb the impact of the anger hurled at him from those who do not believe what he has to say about Jesus. And mind you, these are not softball tosses landing on his head, chest, back, limbs, and other parts of his body. I imagine the religious zealots clutching stones, winding up like a modern-day pitcher, and throwing a fastball right at Stephen.

As each strike brings Stephen closer to death, Stephen kneels down and screams: "Lord, do not hold this sin against them." (Acts 7:60)

A wrongly accused, convicted, and abused follower of the Risen Christ is not asking, but demanding his God to forgive those who have brought him to his knees. Stephen can do this because he keeps sight of the transcendent God in the midst of life's tribulations. He knows that as important as this life is, this life is not all there is.

Stephen sounds a lot like Jesus on the Cross who prayed on behalf of the soldiers who crucified him: "Father, forgive them; for they do not know what they are doing." (Luke 23:34)

If the Christian Church is to have any influence outside its sanctuaries (let alone inside), it must always keep sight of God's transcendence so that it can extend forgiveness.

***

Remember the murders of nine people at the Emanuel AME Church in Charleston, South Carolina? And do you remember how the survivors confronted the racist who carried out the attack?

Because of their Resurrection faith, they extended forgiveness.

And if forgiveness can be extended in such an extreme situation, what about on a mundane, everyday level: when a waiter at a restaurant spills drinks on me, or someone cuts me off in traffic, or someone close to me betrays me? Can I forgive, knowing I am in as much need of forgiveness as those who wrong me?

Can I give up the anger I have in me, as well as the desire for revenge, so that God can begin what is oftentimes the slow and long work of healing and reconciliation?

Some say the act of UNFORGIVENESS is like drinking poison and expecting the other person to die.

But how does a Christian's extension of forgiveness in the face of wrongdoing influence those around us?

As Stephen is about to be murdered, Luke tells us that the witnesses of Stephen's killing placed their coats at the feet of a young man named Saul. This is Saul of Tarsus, also known as Paul. Saul is a

Hebrew name, but since his father was a Roman citizen, Saul was also a Roman citizen by birth, and thus had a Latin name: Paul.

Saul is close enough to the execution that he can hear the stones hitting Stephen's body. But he is also close enough to hear Stephen's scream, Stephen's prayer for God to forgive his murderers.

And while Saul initially approves of Stephen's killing by religious authorities, we can wonder how Stephen's extension of forgiveness in the face of death made Saul think.

How many times did Saul replay this tragedy in his mind to examine why Stephen did what he did?

The episode must have been in the back of Saul's mind as he was breathing out murderous threats against followers of the Way, looking for more Jesus followers to kill.

It is a hunt on the Road to Damascus when the Risen Christ appears to Saul… Saul is blinded by God's transcendence… and Saul is converted from religious terrorist to follower of Jesus.

Did Stephen's act of forgiveness influence someone he did not know, someone he could not have expected to be listening to his voice? Did Stephen's act of faith open up the door for another to see and receive the Risen Christ?

I believe it did.

May we have the grace like Stephen to keep our eyes on God's eternal purpose, and forgive every time we are wronged.

Alleluia! Christ is Risen!
The Lord is Risen Indeed! Alleluia!

Politics and Religion

Homily for May 28, 2017

It is Memorial Day weekend in the United States of America. A time when, as stated in *The Book of Common Prayer*, we remember before God with grateful hearts "… the men and women of our country who in the day of decision ventured much for the liberties we now enjoy" (page 839).

The longer I am ordained, and the more I hear and learn from veterans in the parish, the more I appreciate how service personnel place themselves on the front lines to help humanity fulfill a key tenet of our Baptismal Covenant: to "… persevere in resisting evil." (BCP 293)

At the same time, I am not immune to the tension American Christians straddle as we navigate two topics some prefer not to discuss in polite company: politics and religion.

Memorial Day weekend, the Fourth of July, and Veterans Day can be times when clergy receive passionate feedback from parishioners. No matter how much or how little patriotic content is included in word, prayer, or hymn, it can be too much for some and not enough for others.

I understand and empathize with each well-reasoned position.

We at St. John's are, in most cases, Americans. Based on my limited experience, there exists here a thoughtful, balanced patriotism, which takes on a variety of expressions. We understand our patriotism in light of the Cross of Christ.

We are first and foremost followers of Jesus.

Our faith informs our patriotism, not the other way around.

Christians are sometimes tempted to view the world from Capitol Hill… when what happens on Capitol Hill should be scrutinized from the hills of Calvary and Olivet… Calvary, because that is where Jesus was crucified… Olivet, because that is where the Risen Christ ascended into heaven.

***

This past Thursday the Church marked the Feast of the Ascension. It was the 40th day of Easter.

In Acts 1:3, St. Luke the Evangelist tells us that Christ Jesus "presented himself alive" to his Apostles and others over the course of forty days after being raised from the dead.

On that 40th day, Jesus ascended to the right hand of God the Father… an event we recall each time we recite the Nicene or Apostles' Creed.

We may have missed church on the 40th day of Easter, but the Ascension of Christ should not be overlooked.

Without question, the Ascension speaks to how Jesus left this earth in a particular way; Christ is not here like he once was.

But the Ascension is NOT about the Risen Christ abdicating his throne as King of kings and Lord of lords.

The Ascension proclaims that the Risen Christ now exercises dominion over the entire cosmos.

***

But what does that look like for us? What are the practical applications of the Ascension?

***

In today's lesson from Acts of the Apostles, the earliest followers of Jesus ask him when HE is going to restore the kingdom to Israel.

When would Christ bring about Israel's political independence?

When would Jesus (a Jew) be a patriot and fix the problems with his nation's government?

It is nowhere in the text, but I sometimes wonder if Jesus was disappointed with his followers right before he ascended into heaven.

Jesus spent three years and forty days with them, teaching them about the true character of God… repentance and forgiveness of sins… how to love God and neighbor… who our neighbor is… how to heal the sick, feed the poor, and clothe the naked… how God raises new life in places we expect death.

And the last question Jesus is asked by his followers is how he might fulfill their political aspirations.

Did those closest to Jesus completely miss his point?

Do those of us who today carry the banner of Christ sometimes miss Jesus' point… cloak ourselves in the trappings of the God… and co-opt Christ as a means to bring about our preferred, political end?

***

Not surprisingly, Jesus does not answer the question in the way his earliest followers might have anticipated.

Instead, Jesus promises to send the Holy Spirit… he vanishes from their sight… and the apostles are stopped dead in their tracks, gazing aimlessly skyward, apparently not knowing what to do next.

Two men in white robes… angels… messengers of God… approach the apostles and ask: Why do you stand looking up toward heaven?

Why do those closest to Jesus not always know where to look for Jesus?

***

At times, I forget God is found in the midst of everyday life. When I doubt God's presence in what I consider to be common or mundane, I put God at a distance. I slip into what could be called an optimistic faith.

An optimistic faith means that while I believe God will ultimately bring about a good result… I am passive about my role as a follower of Jesus; I am content to stand around, think God is not close, and yet wonder when God will come down and fix all of my problems.

When faith is reduced to optimism, the Christian life (if we can call it that any longer) becomes a spectator sport.

***

When we read about the Apostles of Jesus in today's lesson, are they mere spectators?

If so, they are not spectators for long… they are not spectators for long because they listen to the angels… they listen to the messengers of God.

"What are you doing?"

"Why are you looking up there and not down here?"

"Why are you waiting on Christ… when you should know by now that Christ has called YOU to take up YOUR cross and follow him?"

"Don't settle for an optimistic faith; embrace a hopeful faith!"

Optimism is passive… hope is active.

Hopeful faith places confidence in the promises of Jesus, even when life and God do not give us the answers we want.

Hopeful faith sees the Ascension of Christ as an INVITATION to PARTICIPATE in God's renewal of creation!

With hopeful faith, WE partner with God to bring order out of chaos… in realms from piety to politics to patriotism… and everything in between.

***

The hopeful faith we embrace because of the Ascension is summed up in the Lord's Prayer… which emboldens us to be God's agents in the world… "… THY kingdom come, thy will be done on earth, as it is in heaven."

The Ascension of Christ is our cue to uncover heaven on earth.

***

Alleluia! Christ is Risen!
The Lord is Risen Indeed! Alleluia!

JUNE

"I will, with God's help"

Homily for June 4, 2017
Pentecost

Today the Church around the world commemorates the feast of Pentecost. The Risen Christ kept and keeps his promise to send the Holy Spirit to his followers. This promise applies not only to the followers of Jesus two thousand years ago. The Holy Spirit is active today, and available to us… and in light of yet another terrorist attack carried out falsely in the name of religion, it is clear we need in our lives the power, presence, and comfort of the Holy Spirit.

In just a moment, we will participate in the baptism of one of the youngest members of the St. John's family. My attention this morning is drawn to a question in the *Book of Common Prayer* posed to… but not limited to… the parents and godparents.

The question: "Will you be responsible for seeing that the child you present (for baptism) is brought up in the Christian faith and life?"

The response: "I will, with God's help."

Notice, there are two elements to the response. When I promise responsibility in passing on the Christian faith and life to my children, as well as other children and adults, there are things I can do. And there are things only God can do through the power of the Holy Spirit.

Communication of the Gospel of Jesus the Christ is a partnership between the divine and the human.

My obligation as a parent, or godparent, or simply as a baptized member of Christ's one, holy, catholic, and apostolic Church, is primarily to be responsible for my own faith.

Do I take part in Eucharistic worship on a consistent basis?

Do I pray daily for myself and others?

Do I engage the heritage of our faith by studying the Scriptures on my own and/or with others in a group?

Do I see Church like Vegas (what happens on Sunday stays on Sunday)? Or is there **integrity** in my faith?

***

The Church has had, and still has, a tremendous impact on my life. And I would say that even if God had not called me to the priesthood. Not everyone is called to the ordained ministry. But all of the baptized are called by God to work in and through the Church, to impact the lives of others for the better, in the name of Jesus.

Like many of you, I have significant memories from childhood which involve the Church.

I recall sitting in the pew next to my mother in the days of the 1928 Prayer Book, a work of art some believe descended directly from the pen of Jesus. While reciting the creedal phrase: From thence he shall come to Judge the quick and the dead… I said to my mother: "I know what 'dead' means, but who are the quick?"

When glancing at the hymnal with my parents, I learned theology of the Church… as well as fundamentals of how to read music.

I think fondly of being awakened from a nap while leaning against my father during church. That evening, he showed me his watch. It read midnight… and while the choir sang, my dad whispered: "Merry Christmas."

My younger sister's baptism is etched in my memory and heart, hopefully the same way George's baptism this morning will be for his older siblings, Ben and Emma.

Many of us have such memories because our parents, or godparents, or people significant in our lives were responsible in their own faith. Even if they were not Episcopalian, they took seriously the "**I will**" element of their call to responsibility.

This is not to say my family growing up… or even my family today with soccer and lacrosse… is going to achieve perfect Sunday attendance. Yes, Sundays are of huge importance in the Christian faith and life. But there is more to God than just one hour on one day out of seven.

We are called to follow Jesus 24/7/365.

We promise: "I will."

Then there is the phrase "… with God's help."

Again, there are things I can do to pass on the Christian faith and life. But only the Holy Spirit can bring someone to faith in Jesus.

Like many of you, there have been seasons in my life apart from the Church.

There are times (still) when I am disillusioned by the institutional church of which I am a part and love fiercely.

There were times, especially in my late teens and early 20s, when I doubted the existence of God, more agnostic than atheist.

I came up with "better ways" to spend a Sunday morning.

At the same time, I knew there was something missing. There was a void in my soul which could not be satisfied by non-church activities I lined up for Sunday mornings.

To make a long story short, I had a strong tug to get back into church.

In retrospect, I had to take responsibility for my own faith. I could no longer ride the coattails of my parents' or godparents' faith.

I had to open myself to the Holy Spirit's activity in my own life.

And that is when Church became more than something to "attend" on a Sunday.

Church became the Body of Christ.

When I took responsibility for my own faith with help from the Holy Spirit, there was a movement away from simply wanting to know things about God.

I wanted to know the God revealed in Jesus of Nazareth.

That happened, and still happens, because people responsible for their own faith stood up on a Sunday morning and proclaimed: "I will, with God's help" ... they followed through on their Sunday morning promise the best they could... and they made room for the Holy Spirit to fill in the gaps.

***

No one can predict how the Holy Spirit will direct a person's life through baptism. But we pray that when the newly baptized come to know Jesus through the power and presence of the Holy Spirit... they will see Church not as something to attend, but a community where they can discover God's purpose for their lives.

May God give us grace to be responsible in our communication of the Christian faith and life… and wisdom to make room for the Holy Spirit.

Alleluia! Christ is Risen!
The Lord is Risen Indeed! Alleluia!

Individuality and Community

Homily for June 11, 2017

It is Trinity Sunday in the Christian Church around the world. We are presented with a math equation we cannot dodge: one equals three; God is both One and Three; God is Father, Son, and Holy Spirit.

Each person of the Trinity is distinctly who He is because He is in relationship with the other persons of the Trinity.

We proclaim our faith in the Triune God each time we recite the Creeds. We see evidence of this God in Scripture, although the word "Trinity" is nowhere to be found.

This church math is evidence of Christians over the centuries seeking to draw closer to the God revealed in Jesus, present now through the Holy Spirit.

We ask questions about the personhood and nature of God because such questions help us learn how to be human.

Since the math can give us fits and starts, it is fair to ask: "How does the Triune God help me in the Christian faith and life?"

Why can we not simply focus on Jesus?

Well, we do focus on Jesus. And when the Church puts a spotlight on the Jesus we meet in the Scriptures, we learn Jesus is both human and divine; one hundred percent man, one hundred percent God; not fifty-fifty.

If it is true that Jesus is both fully human and fully divine, we then have to ask: how is that possible? And that question prompts us to ask a new set of inquiries about how Jesus relates to the Father and the Holy Spirit.

This is key. Within God's self, within the God-head, God lives in relationship. God is already a community: Father, Son, and Holy Spirit.

And it is through God the Son, Jesus, that God draws us into the Divine Community.

So when Jesus calls us to follow him and become part of humanity's dance with the Divine, Jesus empowers us to extend the invitation of Divine Community to others.

We are called to the difficult, counter-cultural task of creating communities which embody the self-giving love Jesus shows for us on the Cross. In creating these communities, we position ourselves to extend and receive the self-giving love each Person of the Trinity has for the other. Such a community is radical, given the hyper-individualistic, me-centered mindset of our day.

When people are approached about becoming part of a community, especially one founded on self-giving love, it can be frightening.

Some are afraid that when they join a church they will be compelled to surrender their identity.

Does following Jesus mean I have to give up my individuality?

I think in our culture we have lost sight of the true understanding of individuality.

We use that word when what we really mean to say is individualism.

Life has become on-demand.

Now, while I receive great pleasure listening to The Who's Greatest Hits on my iPhone while working in the yard, isolating myself in an individualistic, on-demand world has its pitfalls.

I can download to my personal device music or TV shows I prefer… binge-watch or listen privately whenever I want… and if I wish to share my thoughts on what I experience in solitude, I go on-line under a pseudonym (protecting the image in which I see myself) to segregated forums… express myself with behavior I am too cowardly to exhibit in person… then not expect to be challenged… and if my view is challenged, I block or report to cyber authorities the person who dared to question me about what I think and how I express it.

I realize that what I just said is both extreme and cynical.

I am NOT saying technology, in and of itself, is bad. But each time humanity comes up with new technologies (printing press, internet, weaponry)… we need to thoughtfully consider how so-called technological "advances" impact the individual and the community.

When we are not careful, we run the risk of allowing technology to define humanity apart from God's intent.

We can become slaves to technology… when technology is meant to serve us.

The truth of this point is played out in Genesis 11, the story about the Tower of Babel.

According to Rabbi Jonathan Sacks, Babel is an allegory about a particular culture which tries to reach new heights without God (they build skyscrapers to the heavens to make a name for themselves).

In building these skyscrapers, the ziggurats of ancient Mesopotamia, the culture overemphasizes human-flourishing and devalues the raw materials of God (they had brick for stone, and bitumen for mortar).

Babel is a cautionary tale about persons in an elitist culture who look down on humans who differ from them (the elitist culture imposes one language with the same words).

When we study Babel, we learn how one segment of humanity refuses to see other humans as being created in the image of God; instead, the elitists look on the so-called "lessers" as commodities to be exploited.

This stark truth about the sin resident in the human condition serves as the basis for current day atrocities like human trafficking, as well as other forms of human-to-human oppression.

The dominant culture in the Tower of Babel story places a premium on a godless, upwardly mobile, uniform humanity.

But this sub-human enterprise… the elevation of individualism… crumbles in the face of the Divine.

What happens in Babel, and what is present to a large degree in the 21st Century, is not representative of the self-giving love we see in the Triune God.

It is not even love.

It is merely self-serving.

It is individualism.

Individualism arises when we isolate ourselves, placing ourselves over and above all others we deem inferior.

Conversely, our individuality surfaces when we engage in Christ-centered (therefore Trinitarian) community.

As we heard in the lesson from the first and second chapters of Genesis, all of humanity is created in the image of God.

We see God's image in Jesus, the Second Person of the Trinity.

We see God's image when we look at each other.

From Jesus, we learn that God lives in relationship. And if God lives in relationship, then those created in the image of God are made to live in relationship, as well.

When we cultivate relationships built on the foundation of the God we know in Jesus... relationships in which we are challenged to give of ourselves freely... we discover our God-given individuality.

Creating a community where this can happen is not for the faint of heart.

It requires vulnerability.

It requires trust in Christ and one another.

But this is part of what it means to be Church: we discover who we are in Christ when we are part of the community created by Christ.

In the name of the Triune God: Father, Son, and Holy Spirit. Amen.

The donkey, the elephant, and the Lamb

Homily for June 25, 2017

Jesus is divisive.

He says so in the passage we just heard from Matthew's gospel.

But I do not want a divisive Jesus… I want the Jesus who brings everybody together!

Christ is about unity, as we shall see.

But Jesus says he is come to set a man against his father, a daughter against her mother, a daughter-in-law against her mother-in-law; and that one's foes will be members of one's own household. And if we do not love Jesus more than other significant people in our lives, we are not worthy of Jesus.

Jesus is divisive.

***

Every so often, I find myself distracted when something both important and difficult is about to take place. It is not that others involved in the task are trying to deceive me. It is not because these people are uncaring or insensitive. It is precisely because they are caring that these distractions come about.

Here is a benign example. When I am in the dental chair, the first thing that happens before my teeth are cleaned is I am asked by the dental tech: what do you want to watch? There is a TV screen mounted to the ceiling. I could watch cable news while getting a root canal. I am not sure which is worse.

When something serious takes place in our lives, we need a soothing distraction… something to soften the blow.

***

I have been searching this week for some sort of distraction when Jesus says he has come not to bring peace, but a sword… a sword not meant for death, but sharp division.

Maybe it is Jesus' voice which softens the blow of his challenging truth.

In this passage, Jesus is not standing in a boat, preaching to those sitting on a hillside. He is not among thousands out in the open. Jesus is with his closest followers. It is an intimate setting. Jesus must be using his voice differently. There is no way Jesus is screaming at the top of his lungs or banging on a podium.

No, with a holy imagination, I hear Jesus in a calm, level, serious tone. His voice comforts as he instructs. No anger, only truth. And the truth which each follower of Jesus has to consider is this:

What priority does Jesus take in my life?

When we answer this question honestly, the Holy Spirit begins his work of division.

Yes, there are a lot of good things in my life, good and great people whom I love. People I would do anything for, people who would do anything for me. There are causes I devote myself to, to better the lives of my family or community.

Each is good. There is nothing fundamentally "bad" about activities in our lives that bring about "good."

But the catch is this: none of the persons or things we consider good is God.

What happens every so often is that we take someone or something "good" … and we give that "good" the place in our lives which should be reserved only for God.

The biblical word for this is idolatry.

One potential "good" I think we are tempted to put in the place of God is government… specifically how individual Christians, as well as entire denominations, can be seduced by partisan politics.

I think I have done a fairly good job to this point of avoiding much, if not all, of the divisive squabbling we hear ad nauseam in the media. But, as your rector… and more importantly as one who endeavors to follow Jesus… I think we need to admit the obvious: partisan politics is hurting our nation.

And that means it is time for all of us to take a fresh look at Jesus… and how the Church's commitment to Jesus can transform Old Town, our surrounding communities, our nation, and the world!

***

Make no mistake. The Church needs to be in the public square to fulfill our Baptismal Covenant… to proclaim the Gospel of Christ, resist evil, advocate for justice, and more.

Government exists to provide substance… and not just lip service… for the health and well-being of its people, defense, infrastructure, economics, civil rights, education, and so much more… this is not an exhaustive list, and I am not a political scientist.

But for government to carry out its role with equity, government's attention must consistently be drawn to the dignity of each and every human being. This is where the Church comes into the picture.

God's Church, using Scripture, Tradition, and Reason when reflecting on the life of Christ, has much to say about how humanity can thrive.

But we silence our own voice when we elevate a donkey or elephant to the place reserved for the Lamb… when we adhere to partisan platforms, and not our Lord's beatitudes and prayer.

It is time for the Church to repent… and reframe the national conversation.

***

Our nation is divided; and many wrongly seek unity from factions responsible for, and who benefit from, such division.

Jesus is divisive. But when we look closely, his division can unite humanity along a spectrum of God-given diversity.

The division of Christ marks the line between what is merely good and who is God.

We must struggle daily to take up our cross and follow Jesus in order to find that line.

***

Are we content to build our lives on a mere good… on fads which fade?

Or do we trust in the eternal Christ… smash the idols we create… and allow God to work through us, the Church, to realize heaven on earth?

JULY

Small Gestures

Homily for July 2, 2017

I fell into a trap this week when attempting to prepare this morning's message. I started this homily several times only to hit "select all" and "delete" for each letter, word, and paragraph I struggled to compose.

Part of the writer's block stemmed from the fact that I was paying too much attention to the National Basketball Association's free-agent signing period, which began yesterday. To me, there is something fascinating about a man in the NBA who makes millions of dollars for putting a ball through a hoop fewer than half the times he shoots it.

I love basketball. It is a fun sport which gets "big-time" attention.

But since I am a church nerd, my fascination with the NBA leads me to philosophical and existential questions like: how do "pro sports" fit into the grand scheme of life?

Why do some in our culture place great value on this kind of competition?

Is the way our culture honors professional athletes out of balance when, as we approach Independence Day, we consider how to honor American service personnel?

And, to take it a bit further, why does Western culture place so much importance on keeping the eye on the prize… climbing the ladders of success… and thinking that the more we have, the more money we make, the more degrees we have on our wall, the more square footage in our houses, the more toys we have to play with… is all of that somehow evidence we are blessed by God?

It is not.

You will hear me say this over and over again: the way of God is not upward mobility, it is downward mobility.

In defiance of the "cotton candy" fed to us by TV preachers: when everything around us tells us our worth comes from being BIG… do we have the courage to be SMALL?

I was so focused on BIG this week … and not focused on the words I was reading in Scripture… that I brought an improper mindset into my sermon preparation. I began looking for something BIG to share with you. After all, listen again to what Jesus says to his first disciples: "Whoever welcomes you welcomes me, and whoever welcomes me welcomes the one who sent me."

Do we understand that?

Whoever welcomes us (followers of Jesus), welcomes Jesus, and when people welcome Jesus, they welcome God the Father.

When we in the Church are who God calls us to be… and we then do what Jesus calls us to do… people encounter God and Jesus when they welcome US into their lives.

Jesus outlines this progression as he is about to send his disciples to the highways and bi-ways.

Earlier in this chapter of Matthew's gospel, we find Jesus empowering his followers to proclaim that God is near.

Jesus implores his disciples to bring physical curing and emotional healing to those who are suffering.

They are to teach people to look for God creating new life, in places folks experience and come to expect death…

… to bring into God's family those whom society has cast out… as well as exorcise powers and principalities which dehumanize persons created in God's image.

Jesus calls us to this huge task.

This is nothing less than world changing!

But the more I read this passage, the more exhausted it made me. What "big" thing must I do to obey Jesus and prove my love for him?

What "grand ministry plan" must I unveil for St. John's… and then how can I motivate you to make it a reality?

Despite the fact that I like to sound intelligent from this pulpit and make clear the complex intricacies of God… as if I have ever done that… something in me resisted the urge to come up with a "big thing" for you and me to do.

I figured out why, when I came across a theologian who had already experienced a struggle similar to mine. And what he learned provides relief for me. He pointed to Jesus' words in the very next sentence: "…whoever gives even a cup of cold water to one of these little ones in the name of a disciple-- truly I tell you, none of these will lose their reward." (Matthew 10:42)

I was searching for God in something big… and I failed to see God in the small.

We can help people discover the Kingdom of Heaven… we can be who Jesus calls us to be and do what Jesus calls us to do… even when we do something as seemingly insignificant as giving someone a cup of cold water.

If we do not hand out a cup of cold water, maybe it is brightening someone's day with our smile… or allowing another car to cut in front of us in traffic… or buying coffee for the person behind us in line at Tim Horton's.

It could be clutching someone's hand when they need… or providing a shoulder to cry on… laughing at a joke… simply saying "thank you" … or holding the door open for someone who doesn't expect it.

Small gestures… but godly, nonetheless.

Theologian William Barclay sums up this morning's gospel lesson the following way:

"The great beauty of this passage is its stress on simple things. The Church and Christ will always need their great orators, their great shining examples of sainthood, their great teachers, those whose names are household words; but the Church and Christ will also always need those in whose homes there is hospitality, on whose hands there is all the service which makes a home, and in whose hearts there is the caring which is Christian love . . . All service ranks the same with God."

May God give us the grace to do something small for Jesus.

Positioning

Homily for July 9, 2017

Last week, as part of a sermon illustration, I made mention of basketball… I drew an analogy to relate basketball to the gospel passage. To be fair, for this week's example, I will reference baseball. Maybe by the end of summer we can touch all major pro sports.

It is funny. There are degrees to which people like baseball. It is known as America's pastime. And when I was growing up, there was the popular phrase: "Baseball, hotdogs, apple pie, and Chevrolet" … likely more popular in Saginaw than Dearborn.

There are people who are die-hard baseball fans. They love it, they sit at home and watch games on TV, or they head to a ballpark to see it in person.

There are folks who will NOT watch baseball on TV, but they have a good time going to a game, like we did last month when we saw the Loons.

And then there are people who, instead of watching baseball, would prefer to watch paint dry.

What brings baseball to mind this week is how a team defends a particular batter. Let us say a batter hits left-handed and he is a pull hitter. That means that more times than not, this batter will put the ball in play somewhere between first and second base. If he hits it out of the infield, the ball will go between right field and center field.

If that is true, the fielders will then position themselves in such a way that gives them a better chance to catch a ball. If a left-handed batter is a dead pull hitter, there are times when even the third baseman on a team will move to the first-based side of second base.

I am so tempted here to recite Abbot and Costello's "Who's on first" routine. But I will not do that.

If this baseball lingo is not helpful, the idea is that the infielders and outfielders go to great lengths to better position themselves to catch the baseball.

***

In today's gospel lesson, Jesus has comforting words for all who will hear: "Come to me, all you that are weary and are carrying heavy burdens, and I will give you rest. Take my yoke upon you and learn from me; for I am gentle and humble in heart, and you will find rest for your souls. For my yoke is easy, and my burden is light."

Jesus speaks truth about the realities of life. Life can beat us down. Life can make us weary. There are events which prompt us to carry the weight of the world on our shoulders.

And let me be clear, the bad things which can happen to us in life are not caused by God. Yes, God created all there is, and God is somehow mysteriously responsible for allowing life to play out as it does (there is a whole discussion which can be had here about humanity's free will).

But God's will for humanity, God's purpose, God's plan… if these words are even adequate… does not include humanity's suffering.

The pain we experience in this life is not God's intent for us. And yet, when we notice all too easily how the suffering is real… life can beat us down.

This is where Jesus comes into the picture… or, at least, this is where Jesus can come into the picture.

Jesus offers us rest for our souls… Jesus invites us to learn from him… and promises to be gentle with us.

But here's the thing. For us to experience the rest Jesus mentions… which would logically follow learning from him and knowing just how humble in heart he is… we must take seriously the first thing Jesus says to us in this sentence.

Jesus says "come to me."

For Jesus to provide the rest that our souls need, for him to relieve our burdens, we must position ourselves in a way similar to a baseball infielder or outfielder.

They ask, where must I stand to catch a baseball?

As followers of Jesus, we ask: where must we stand to receive God?

***

You have heard me say it before, and I will say it again… and I say this because I am growing to love all of you and this parish deeply. I want you to know the truth I have discovered in my life as an Episcopal Christian.

My hope for you is not that you become a "church-goer" … one who checks off the religion box every so often by "attending" a church service… one whose commitment level to St. John's is similar to that of a service club.

My hope for you is that you become… or more deeply engage your identity as… a disciple of THE God who became human in Jesus and is present with us now through the Holy Spirit.

Discipleship includes… but is not limited to… Sunday.

Following Jesus is as much about Monday through Saturday as it is about Sunday.

So the question becomes:

What do we do Monday through Saturday to position ourselves to learn from Jesus… experience his gentleness… and find rest for our souls?

Over the years, I have found… and I am sure many of you have found… that our daily devotional practices change. There are days, weeks, and months when our souls are fed by the Daily Office found in the *Book of Common Prayer*. And there are seasons when our spirit craves something else.

Recently, my soul began craving something else. So, I am now again working a "daily bible" … over the course of the next year, I will read through the entire bible. Each day there is a section from the Old Testament, the Psalms, Proverbs, and the New Testament. This is feeding my soul right now. And this particular devotion takes about fifteen minutes a day.

I will put the link to this book and a few other devotions on the St. John's website for you to consider.

The challenge is straightforward: what do our souls need?

And are we willing to position ourselves in such a way to receive God?

I recently heard a saying that each follower of Jesus is a work in progress… but we still have to work at our progress.

Jesus says: "Come to me, all you that are weary and are carrying heavy burdens, and I will give you rest. Take my yoke upon you, and learn from me; for I am gentle and humble in heart, and you will find rest for your souls. For my yoke is easy, and my burden is light."

Unforced Errors

Homily for July 16, 2017

If you would humor me for a few moments, I would like to continue with a theme I started by accident. Each of the past two Sundays, I have illustrated the gospel passages by referencing a particular sport.

Last week we spoke of baseball, two weeks ago it was basketball. This week, I would like to try tennis.

This came to mind last Sunday afternoon while watching coverage of Wimbledon, the annual tennis tournament held at the All England Lawn Tennis and Croquet Club in London.

Wimbledon introduced me to the term fortnight. That is how long it lasts. Fortnight means "fourteen nights," or two weeks. So, I think today is the last day for Wimbledon 2017.

Tennis has a unique way of scoring. Instead of marking points as 0, 1, 2, 3, or 4… there is Love, 15, 30, 40, Deuce, and Advantage… not to mention that a player has to win a certain number of games within a set, and a certain number of sets within a match.

There are aces, faults, double faults, lets… as well as confusing sets of lines on the court which make sense only when one realizes said lines are for doubles matches and not singles.

In tennis, as with other sports, there is the concept of an unforced error. An unforced error in tennis occurs during what is considered to be a normal rally… a normal volley… and, for whatever reason, a player loses a point by hitting "out of bounds" (or into the net) a ball that, in the judgment of others, was easily playable.

The opponent did not do anything spectacular to win the point; the player who lost the point simply made a mistake.

My brief high school tennis career, in and of itself, was an unforced error.

***

In today's gospel lesson, Jesus talks to his disciples about what sometimes happens when we encounter the word of the kingdom… meaning moments when God breaks into our lives.

Jesus makes his point by telling a parable, a story.

Jesus talks about God in agricultural terms… how God is a sower who plants seed… and God is seemingly wasteful with the seed… God scatters this seed everywhere… and God does not stop scattering the seed.

God is both persistent and patient when it comes to having the kingdom of heaven grow in our lives.

In tennis terms, God lobs the ball over the net easily so that we can make contact with it… and God does so to help us prepare for what life can hit our way.

But… from time to time… when we are confronted with the word of God, we commit unforced errors.

Jesus says, in effect, there are unforced errors we commit when God scatters seed in our direction: lack of understanding… lack of depth… fear… and indifference.

Last week, I spoke about the need to position ourselves to hear from God… to make time to engage Scripture to learn and UNDERSTAND who God is.

I have found in ministry that those of us in the institutional Church can sometimes be described as a group of "cut flowers." That is from a quotation attributed to English lay theologian G.K. Chesterton.

There is beauty in cut flowers. But cut flowers, by definition, are separated from the root. And once something is separated from its roots, it is only a matter of time before it dies.

A Church can get so caught up in practices not central to the Gospel of Jesus Christ… that it can lose focus and separate from its roots.

When we fail to study the Scriptures, when we do not constantly remind ourselves who God is and what God's mission in Christ is, we forget who we are.

We lose understanding of both God and ourselves.

When that happens, there is no depth to our faith. And from a posture of nominalism… because we are confused about conviction and allegiance… we seek validation from individuals and organizations other than God.

On a personal level, we become afraid that no one will love and affirm us, so… out of fear… we conform ourselves to the whims of others. But when we do that, over the long haul, we come up empty.

Every single time.

This is how an unforced error unfolds in the Christian life. It comes from a lack of focus, a lack of discipline.

Jesus tells us this story to remind us to be disciplined, to be his disciples.

There are times in our lives when God scatters seed our way… and without discipline, we fail to understand what God wants for us and seeks from us.

Without discipline, we fear what God tells us.

Fear of God's word causes us to step back from anything that has to do with God… and when we intentionally step back from God, we become indifferent to God.

Jesus cautions us not to fall into this cycle.

Jesus calls us to be good soil… to actively listen for what God has to tell us… to struggle to understand, especially when understanding does not come easily… because when we struggle, it is a good thing.

In the struggle, we prepare ourselves in such a way that God's seed can take root… and when God's seed takes root in us, we blossom in the way God desires.

In the name of God: Father, Son, and Holy Spirit. Amen.

Hubris and Humility

Homily for July 23, 2017

It seems there is some friendly wagering taking place in the parish. The question: what sport will be referenced this week as we unpack the Gospel lesson? Thus far, we have examined basketball, baseball, and tennis.

Today, I am not going to speak about one sport in particular. Instead, I would like to explore my experiences as a parent of children who play "little league" sports.

I will not stand here and lament how too many families spend Sunday mornings at sporting events and not at church.

I think the institutional Church casts too many stones in that direction.

With a non-critical mind, Christian leaders sometimes blame the nebulous category of "sport" for all that is wrong with the Church (or America) today.

At the core, there is nothing wrong with children playing sports, working over the years for a college scholarship, and hoping to play sports on a professional level.

Can a sport become idolatrous? Yes, just like any other good thing.

But what I have noticed within myself is an attitude which rears its ugly head every time I attend a game my children play in. I want to call this attitude what it is: sin. It is a posture which tempts me to villainize players, coaches, and parents who wear a different uniform.

We are all guilty of this on some level, with sports or other activities. For whatever reason, it is become acceptable to refuse to see the "good" in someone who holds opinions different than mine. They must be evil, backward thinking, and sinful.

I wrongly choose self-serving hubris over Christ-like humility.

Again, it is not endemic to sports. We see this mentality in business, government, and other parts of society.

This is precisely why the temptation for people to elevate themselves at the expense of others is all throughout Scripture.

This sin exists in the Church, as well. Too much of American Christianity is reduced to who is going to heaven and who is not. I'm in, you're out.

But that is not how we in the Episcopal Church understand the coming of God's kingdom.

***

In this morning's gospel passage, Jesus explains to anyone who will listen what the kingdom of heaven is like.

In other words, what is life like not when the political party of our choosing controls all three branches of government?

What is life like when it dawns on us that Jesus is in charge?

Jesus says the kingdom of heaven is like a field in which someone sows "good seed" in a Master's field. And while nobody is looking an enemy sows "weeds" among the "wheat" … there is bad in the midst of good.

In their zeal, the Master's slaves… when they notice what they deem to be corruption…become fearful… and plan to violently purify their Master's field. They intend to root out the weeds from the wheat.

The Master's minions seek to eliminate those they consider OTHER; they envision a future of being surrounded only by those who are like them.

Tell me that does not happen today… tell me some who raise the flag of Christianity do not root out people considered "of the enemy."

This goes in each direction – so-called progressives and conservatives do this to each other.

Maybe this in-fighting is what keeps people out of church of Sundays. People recognize this behavior for what it is: non-Christian.

We do this with social media, too. We "friend" or "follow" only those we like. We block, restrict, mute, or unfollow those we choose to hate.

But in Jesus' parable, the Master tells his slaves not to come to his defense on his first-century timeline: Do not attempt to purify my field. Do not launch a crusade to root out the weeds… if you do, you will destroy wheat in the process.

***

Let us circle back to me as a little league parent. When my children are on an athletic field… because they are my children… and because they wear a particular jersey, I have a vested interest in what is mine. That means I stand in opposition to those affiliated with the other team. I am wheat, they are weeds.

On the other sideline, might there be parents who have a similar mindset… only their children are wheat, and mine are weeds?

How can we distinguish between wheat and weeds when we define those terms from our own perspectives and not God's?

If we act on our own devices apart from God, we destroy not only weeds… but wheat. This is sin.

What are we to do?

In Jesus' parable, the Master tells his servants to let the weeds grow with the wheat. The Master will sort it all out at the harvest.

What do we make of this?

Some look at this passage and say those who are evil… those whom they deem to be evil… those whom they consider as other… will be cast into the fires of hell for eternity.

I'm going to heaven, you're not.

But that is not how I read this passage anymore.

What I understand is that at the harvest… at the end of this age… when I come face-to-face with God, God's refining fire will burn away the weeds… the sin nature I have cultivated in my life.

There will be "weeping and gnashing of teeth" on my part because, standing before God, I will be confronted with the "things done" and "left undone," as we say in the General Confession.

I am thankful Jesus will be standing next to me during that process so that I can face up to the wrong I have done… repent… receive perspective… and make amends so that I am able to live eternally with the Father.

***

Jesus' explanation about the end of this age should impact how we live during this age.

When in this life we are tempted to play the game of "us" versus "them" … to demonize those we consider "different" … may God give us the grace to admit that each of us is a mixture of both wheat and weeds… and with the help of Christ Jesus, we opt for humility over hubris… and when we do that, the Church embraces its mission to usher in the kingdom of heaven.

A W.W.E. Christmas

Homily for July 30, 2017

We continue this morning examining the Good News of Jesus Christ by seeking analogies through sports. If you are keeping score, to date we have examined basketball, baseball, tennis, and the pitfalls of being a little league parent.

Today, we enter what could be considered the "gray area" of athletic competition. There are times when people sit around and debate the legitimacy of a particular sport or the athleticism of an individual. Such can be the case with professional wrestling.

Tonight at the Dow Events Center, WWE (World Wrestling Entertainment) puts on a show. My son Cade and I have tickets. You heard me right, your rector spent money to attend a professional wrestling event.

I am actually looking forward to this. Some of you have told me WWE always puts on a good SHOW. And you emphasize the word SHOW. WWE is nothing like high school or college wrestling, which is competition in the true sense of the word.

But we have to ask: what is professional wrestling?

Let's be real, St. John's! Who on this planet could actually survive a backbreaker, or brain-buster, a choke-slam, cutter, DDT (I don't even know what that is), face-buster, neck-breaker, or pile-driver.

This is NOT to say those who take part in professional wrestling are any less athletic, any less talented. I do not want to tangle with anyone affiliated with the WWE. But I do want to be entertained. I know what professional wrestling is not, and I know what it is. I gladly accept it for what it is: a show.

In this morning's gospel passage, Jesus peppers us with several one or two-line parables of what the kingdom of heaven is like.

The parable which stands out to me today is this one: Jesus says "… the kingdom of heaven is like a merchant in search of fine pearls; on finding one pearl of great value, he went and sold all that he had and bought it."

So, in this one-sentence parable, Jesus speaks of a merchant. A merchant, of course, is a store-keeper… a retailer… one who makes a profit through the purchase and eventual sale of an item. In this case, it is pearls.

The pattern is this: a merchant has to spend money to make money… the merchant has to sell the item for more money than she or he spent on the item… so, to do that, it is likely that the merchant has to come up with a sales pitch.

American merchants spend a lot of money on the sales pitch. Corporate America puts on a SHOW to make us think we need the product they have to sell… and we pay attention to these shows.

If I were to ask you to draw the logos for McDonald's, or Mercedes Benz, or Apple Computers, you could do it. We resonate with the show.

***

But something happens to the merchant in the middle of Jesus' short parable. Someone whose life-work it is to purchase and "sell-with-a-show" comes across ONE pearl of great value. This one pearl is different than the hundreds or thousands of other pearls encountered by the experienced merchant.

When the merchant learns of this pearl, he realizes that his days as a retailer are near an end. Instead of leading a life of acquisition in order to dispense for personal profit… the merchant changes his practice 180-degrees. The soon to be former merchant dispenses of everything he owns, all he once gave ultimate importance… and takes to himself the newly-discovered pearl of great value.

Jesus says when we discover the kingdom of heaven for what it is… how the God who forms the universe also creates us, loves us far more than we can imagine, and prepares a place for us eternal in the heavens through Christ Jesus… our heart-felt response is like that of the merchant.

When we take to heart that God is close to us in Jesus, our priorities change. Instead of looking to religious institutions for a show, or shopping for a Church which caters to my demographic, I approach a worship service with the desire to spend time with God and God's people.

I go to church because, when faithful and when flawed, it is the oyster which gives to the world the pearl of great value.

***

Last Sunday, the Hallmark Channel ended its two-week run of Christmas movies in July. After all, "Christmas in July" is part of our culture, right? More often than I care to admit, my family and I gathered around the TV this month to watch these completely cheesy, made-for-TV holiday flicks.

These movies generally center on rich, happy, good-looking people who have existential crises while working corporate jobs in the big city. They long for the so-called simpler times of growing up in a small, Midwestern town, even though they have repressed the reasons they left home in the first place.

The main characters of these movies enter a magical world after slipping on the ice or falling off a step-ladder while putting a star atop a Christmas tree… and they encounter angelic characters who take them on a journey of shallow reflection.

Each of the central characters comes to the realization that she or he would have lived life differently if given the opportunity to do so. And because it is the Hallmark channel, they get their second chance... snow begins to fall... and everybody lives happily ever after.

I tell you, if this priest thing doesn't work out, I'm going to work for the Hallmark Channel.

I watch a lot of these movies. Apparently, they fill some sort of void in my life. But here's the thing: it's just entertainment.

These movies give us winter weather without complication... Christmas trees which need no care... presents/gifts we do not regret when the bills arrive in January... family reunions without major conflict... home-cooked Holiday dinners from five-star restaurants... low-cost motivations to be kinder at the office... a low-risk escape from the rat race to follow my heart and become a wildlife photographer in Alaska... and where the North Pole is depicted as some sort of promised land where elves are well-rested, peace-filled, and do not mind the fact that they are workaholics.

Do you know what each of these shows leaves out? The pearl of great price.

They sell us on the sizzle. But they never give us the steak.

They give us Christmas without Christ.

Each of these movies places at its center important concepts of life. But they leave out the Christ who Himself is the Way, the Truth, and the Life.

As we go about our lives in the Church and the world... do we want a show... or do we seek an encounter with the living God who reveals Himself to us in Jesus?

AUGUST

Up North

Homily for August 6, 2017

This summer, you introduced me to a phrase I had not heard before moving to Michigan. I think this phrase fits in well with our practice of looking for analogies in sports as we dig into the Gospel of Jesus Christ. The phrase in question brings to mind the outdoors: lakes, boats, hiking, kayaking, and so much more.

The phrase: "Up North!"

When I hear "Up North," it has a ring of mysticism to it… there is a sense of ascending to a different level.

It seems no matter where a Michigander lives, she or he heads "up north" at some point during the summer for vacation, for outdoor sports and recreation.

I love the word "recreation" … it literally means "re-creation" … to create again. It draws our attention to the first verses of Genesis, in which God brings the created order into being… and on the seventh day, God rested… God is not a workaholic.

This is the point behind the Sabbath, the day of rest. From the Genesis story, humanity is to learn that we are not robots; we were not put on this earth simply to be defined by our work, our production, that which we create. We are to take time away from work, our doing, reflect upon what it is we do on a daily basis, rediscover the BEING which undergirds what we do, behold God's good creation, and in doing that, we can be re-created.

There is just something about being pulled out of "everyday life" which allows us to find godly perspective on "everyday life."

I wonder if that is the case for three of Jesus' disciples in today's gospel lesson. We are invited on a walk with Jesus and some of his closest followers: Peter, James, and John. Each of these disciples is a fisherman. They did not fish for sport, as far as we can tell. They fished to support their families.

On this occasion, Jesus takes a group of fishermen mountain-climbing.

Many important encounters with God in the Bible take place on a mountain. Abraham nearly sacrificed his son Isaac on Mount Moriah… Moses received the Ten Commandments on Mount Sinai… the prophet Elijah had a showdown with the prophets of Baal on Mount Carmel.

With that backdrop, Peter, James, John, and we have a mountain-top experience this morning with Jesus. Scholars are not sure exactly which mountain this is. It could have been Mount Tabor, which has an elevation of about 1800-feet. It could have been Mount Hermon, elevation 9200-feet. In either case, it is quite the change of scenery for Peter, James, and John… fishermen from the Sea of Galilee… elevation: 695-feet BELOW sea level.

Jesus, Peter, James, and John climb the mountain for a specific reason: to pray. They distance themselves from other disciples. They put space between themselves and the hustle and bustle of the cities to which they travel.

And they hold this prayer meeting at the point in Luke's gospel following Peter's declaration that Jesus is God's Messiah… Jesus is the focal point of God's rescue mission for all of humanity… Jesus is the person in whom heaven and earth meet… and God's mission in Jesus will be accomplished not through military might, as some Jews were expecting from their coming Messiah. No, God's mission in Jesus would be accomplished through the death and resurrection of Jesus.

This is a lot for anybody to comprehend, which may be why Jesus, Peter, James, and John go on retreat.

As they pray, Jesus' face is transfigured; it is changed some way. Luke does not tell us exactly how. But I think of times when I look at someone familiar, and I notice something about that person I had not seen before.

And it is not just Jesus' face which is altered… his clothes become dazzling white.

So what does this mean? Theologians talk about the "height and light" of Jesus' transfiguration.

They ascend a mountain… they reach new heights in their journey with God… and while Jesus is still every bit what the disciples experienced before this moment, they see him in a new light… they receive clarification about his identity… they have a mystical experience… and now understand Jesus as a human being, and as God in human flesh.

Moses and Elijah appear… these are two prominent figures in the history of God's people… they speak with Jesus about what Jesus would accomplish on a mountain outside of Jerusalem.

Now, Luke makes a point to tell us that Peter, James, and John are exhausted. What happens when we are exhausted? We let our guard down, we become vulnerable, we are more accepting of what is going on around us… in a passive way.

All of this is to say that when Peter, James, and John experience Jesus in a new way, it is not something they manufacture. We cannot manipulate God's activity in our lives. But when we endeavor to stay awake and alert with Jesus... even when doing so becomes tiring... we open ourselves to a deeper experience with Jesus.

Peter is exhausted… but when Peter discovers this new dimension of Jesus, Peter is energized to make this experience permanent. He wants to build three dwellings, three tents, three tabernacles.

Tabernacle is an important word in the Bible.

Tabernacles are structures the Israelites used in the wilderness during their Exodus from Egypt. In a mystical sense, it is a reminder that God is close to us… even during what we might consider to be desert, or spiritually dry, experiences of our lives.

With the tabernacles, the Israelites know they are at home with God once they escape life under Pharaoh... and before they settle in the land God promised them.

In the prologue of John's Gospel, we are told that the Word (Christ Jesus) became flesh and lived among us… taken literally, God became a human being in Jesus and "tabernacled" with us (John 1:14).

On the mountain in today's gospel lesson, God's dwelling with humanity in Jesus is confirmed with the words of the Father, heard by Peter, James, and John… and spoken to us this morning and every day. The Father says: "This is my Son, my chosen; listen to him."

God speaks these words right before the "mountaintop experience" comes to an end… there is clarity and purpose about Jesus when time "Up North" for Peter, James, and John is over… and that is as it should be.

***

We can learn much from our time "Up North" … from spiritual retreats… from re-creation… from mountaintop experiences.

Such moments are all too rare and fleeting… yet precious.

But when we… like Peter, James, and John… remove ourselves from the idolatry of busyness and productivity, we give ourselves a chance to see Jesus in a new light.

We make ourselves available to receive strength from Christ to live down the mountain… on ground level… each and every day of our lives.

Jesus, the Chosen, and the Dogs

Homily for August 20, 2017

Does the God of the Bible favor one race over all others?

Does God call for the genocide of those not part of the chosen race?

And if the answer to each of these questions is 'yes,' then why would I want to model my life on the values of this God?

The questions I raise are asked often when persons read the Hebrew Scriptures, what we Christians call the Old Testament… especially when it comes to interactions between the Israelites and the Canaanites.

These questions are addressed thoughtfully in videos from a group called The Bible Project. I will post links to these videos on the St. John's website when I post the audio of this sermon. The background picture I am about to paint draws heavily from The Bible Project.

We remember in Scripture how Moses led the Israelites out of bondage in Egypt, set out for the Promised Land, yet wandered in the wilderness for forty years. While in the wilderness, God gave instructions on what the Israelites were to do as they entered the Promised Land: wipe out the Canaanites, people of a different race, ethnicity, and culture who inhabited the land before the Israelites.

The Canaanites were seen as a morally corrupt populace who, among other things, practiced child-sacrifice.

Canaanites were descendants of Noah's son Ham.

The name Ham, translated from Egyptian, can mean "heat," or "burnt," or "sunburnt," or "black."[3]

Ham saw Noah naked after Noah got drunk following the flood… an action frowned upon in the ancient world, to say the least.

---

[3] http://www.biblestudytools.com/dictionary/ham/

From this event comes the Curse of Ham, which falls on Ham's son Canaan and Canaan's descendants.

This bible story gave rise to RACIST theologies.

This racist theology is still adhered to today by certain groups of Christians in the United States of America.

This understanding of Scripture, when held up to the Jesus we meet in Scripture, is simply false.

***

Let us consider the question: would God order the genocide of the Canaanites or any group of people?

That can be easily understood when reading the book of Joshua.

I adhere to the interpretation that God did NOT order the elimination of the Canaanites, since shortly after God supposedly calls on the Israelites to obliterate the Canaanites, God instructs them not to marry or enter into business dealings with the Canaanites.

This violates the law of noncontradiction. How can one marry or conduct business with a Canaanite after exterminating them?

So, what gives?

Scholars say the supposed commands from God to destroy Canaan are hyperbole, extreme (non-literal) statements from the biblical authors intended to make a point.

The point of the biblical authors is that the Israelites are not to be influenced by an immoral culture… immoral NOT because of external appearance; but because of internal affinities.

God's people are to speak truth to surrounding cultures and subcultures… pointing others to the one, true God.

In the land promised to the Israelites, some Canaanites… like Rahab the Prostitute, as well as the Gibeonites... DID come to honor God.

***

In this morning's gospel lesson, we witness an interaction between Jesus (a Jew) and a Canaanite woman.

We know there were cultures in Jesus' time which viewed women as little more than property of men… a fact which makes this story, and many other stories in the Bible, so much more remarkable. And we know the contentious history between Jews and Canaanites.

Listen to the desperation in the Canaanite woman's voice as she gets close to Jesus. Look at the stress in her face, the tears in her eyes, the way her body trembles. She calls Jesus by his proper, Messianic Jewish title… and she begs for mercy.

Life has become too much to bear, and she wants Jesus to lift a burden. She does not come asking for herself, she presents herself before Jesus on behalf of her daughter who is tormented by a demon. We are not told what that demon is, but we can imagine, since we all have our demons.

The Canaanite woman makes her opening argument before Jesus, and she is ignored.

With 21st century American eyes we might ask:

Is she ignored because she is a woman?

Is it because she is "black"?

***

Full disclosure: Jesus was not white… but he had darker skin than mine, and probably lighter skin than the Canaanite woman.

***

JESUS... God in human flesh, the Savior of the World.... is silent in the face of this "black" woman and her daughter's problem.

What is going on here?

Is Matthew's description of Jesus interacting with the Canaanite woman conveyed as a non-literal, hyperbolic way to make a larger point?

Or is Emmanuel, "God with us," deciding not to be with some of us?

If being ignored is not bad enough, the male disciples of Jesus… those closest to him… implore Jesus to send away this Canaanite woman. After all, she's shouting. She's not quiet. And she is not going to be silenced. She embodies the quotation: "Well-behaved women seldom make history."

This Canaanite woman is not only making history… but we have to wonder if she is about to remind Jesus about God's history with the Jewish people and where it is leading.

When the disciples cry louder for Jesus to dismiss this woman, Jesus says he has come only for the lost sheep of the house of Israel.

Jesus' statement is either exclusive or particular.

If Jesus' statement is exclusive, then God became flesh only for the benefit of the Jewish people. If Jesus' statement is particular, then God became flesh in Jesus (a Jew) for the world's benefit.

Which is it? And why is Jesus acting this way toward the Canaanite woman?

The disciples step up their efforts to get rid of this woman… but she throws herself to the ground before Jesus and begs: "Lord, help me!"

But Jesus tells the woman it is not fair to take the children's food and throw it to the dogs.

Did Jesus just call this woman a dog?

The Canaanite woman is not deterred. In fact, she shows us just how sharp and theological her mind is. She says to Jesus: "... even the dogs eat the crumbs that fall from their master's table."

The Canaanite woman knows that what God is doing in Jesus is not for a privileged few.

The Canaanite woman has faith that even a scrap of God's grace… falling from the table like manna from heaven... will benefit her troubled daughter.

Jesus' mission to the Israelites is a blessing for the entire world.

We learn of this early on in the Book of Genesis in God's call to Abram… the call which culminates in Jesus. God says to Abram: "I will make of you a great nation, and I will bless you, and make your name great, so that you will be a blessing." (Genesis 12:2)

The Canaanite woman knows how God blesses all nations in Jesus… and she gravitates to Jesus in her time of need.

Jesus is impressed by this woman's faith… and the woman's daughter is healed instantly… the God of the Bible shows favor to Canaanites, those once considered to be enemies.

***

I hesitate to say if, in this story, Jesus learned something new about his mission, was reminded of it, or was acting in a certain way so others could learn.

In any case, again or for the first time, we learn something from a woman of color whom some believe to be condemned by God.

The Canaanite woman proclaims the truth of God's salvation offered to all in Jesus.

God became flesh in Jesus to gather the lost sheep of the house of Israel. And in doing that, God brings healing to all nations of the world.

God's disclosure to us in Christ is meant NOT ONLY for a small number of so-called chosen ones.

When God blesses a particular group of people, that particular group should then become a blessing to all of those around them… because while we have distinct features on the OUTSIDE... INSIDE, as well as outside, each of us is created in the image of God.

Spectator or Participant?

Homily for August 27, 2017

This morning, we are invited on a field trip with Jesus. He has taken his followers to the district of Caesarea Philippi. When I visited the Holy Land more than seventeen years ago, this was one of the stops on the pilgrimage. There we reflected on the passage from Matthew's gospel which we just heard.

Today's story takes place in the ancient Israelite city of Paneas. But since the Promised Land was under the control of the Roman Empire, many places had Roman names.

This area was named after Caesar. But since there was already a Caesarea not too far from Paneas, Herod Philip (who might be considered a real estate developer for the district) added his own name. Thus, Caesarea Philippi.[4]

Caesarea Philippi was described by our tour guide as a religious supermarket. In Caesarea Philippi, you could find a temple to just about any god you wanted to worship.

The Canaanites there built a temple to the pagan god Baal, whom we read about in the Old Testament. Baal was a fertility god… farmers turned to Baal for crops, people turned to Baal for children.

The Greeks and Romans built sanctuaries because of the cave of Pan.[5] Pan was the god of the wild from Greek mythology.[6]

---

[4] http://www.bible-history.com/geography/ancient-israel/caesarea-philippi-paneas.html

[5] http://www.bible-history.com/biblestudy/caesarea-philippi.html

[6] https://greekgodsandgoddesses.net/gods/pan/

As I remember it, Caesarea Philippi is a beautiful place: stone mountains (or hills) and fast-moving streams running through the middle of it all.

Let us picture this in our minds. We are standing next to the disciples. We are looking at Jesus, Jesus is looking at us. Behind Jesus is Caesarea Philippi in all its glory.

If we take our eyes off Jesus, we might be able to look at the temple of Baal or the sanctuaries of Pan.

As our eyes move from Jesus, to Baal, to Pan, and back to Jesus… Jesus asks us a question:

"Who do people say that the Son of Man is?"

Jesus refers to himself with a term we need to understand: Son of Man. It is a direct quotation from the Book of Daniel (7:13).

The best way for us to define the term is this: the Son of Man is the prototype for humanity.

In Jesus, we see God's intent for humanity, both individually and collectively.[7]

Even though Jesus asks a question here, he makes a statement about himself.

Jesus proclaims that he is the Messiah whom God desired to send to the Jewish people and humanity all along.

Jesus plants a flag, and he wants feedback from his followers… first about what other people have to say about him.

---

[7] https://cac.org/abstract-to-personal-2016-10-26/

The disciples provide Jesus with a set of answers that OTHERS were giving about Jesus... others compare Jesus to some well-known Jewish prophets, or to a popular religious leader of Jesus' day: John the Baptist.

Jesus then adjusts the question. Now that he has heard what others have said about him, Jesus wants to know what his own followers see in him.

"... who do you say that I am?"

Simon Peter gives the right answer. Jesus is the Messiah, the Son of the living God. Jesus praises Peter... and goes on to say that the faith Peter has articulated will serve as the foundation for the mission of the Church.

As is the case with any sermon or bible study, there are many different directions we could go here. But what has been front and center in my mind this week are the two questions Jesus poses in this passage.

What do others think about me? What do you think about me?

Jesus' questions move his followers from passivity to activity... from spectator to participant.

***

For most of the summer, I supplemented sermons by looking for analogies in sports. Given all that has taken place in our nation in recent weeks, I did not feel like I could do that in last Sunday's sermon. There is a risk of sounding glib or flippant with analogies, which always fall short of what I am attempting to describe.

But today, I cannot escape my excitement with the beginning of the college football season.

I have not always been a fan of football. In fact, I did not become a football fan until the fall of 1987, my freshman year at East Carolina

University in Greenville, North Carolina. I became a football fan because I was in the marching band, and we had to be at every home game… and there was a road-trip to NC State mixed in.

I marched at the University of North Texas, as well, after transferring there.

Now, I was in the marching band in high school. But I did not even think to like football, because my high school band somehow came to view football with disdain. We left the games after we performed at halftime. We did not really have that much pride when it came to the football team. So, I was not a football fan in high school.

But when I got to college, everything changed. College Football Saturday is a liturgy unto itself. The band, the cheerleaders, the fans, and, oh yeah, the football team.

There is something about the colors and the pageantry which speak to us on levels which are different than professional sports.

I came to love football… because I came to love everything about College Football Saturdays… and I came to love College Football Saturdays because I was in the band, I was involved. I was not simply a spectator, I was a participant.

***

When Jesus asks us two questions about his identity and mission, he is really asking one question.

Who do others say that I am? Who do you say that I am?

Both of these questions lead us to ask:

When we come to see Jesus as God's blueprint for humanity, how meaningful would it be to participate in making God's plan for the world a reality?

SEPTEMBER

Selfie Denial

Homily for September 3, 2017

We find ourselves in the middle of a conversation which began last week. Jesus and his disciples are still in Caesarea Philippi. In response to a question from Jesus, Peter has rightly stated that Jesus is the Messiah, the Son of the living God.

One point we did not address last week is that Jesus told his followers not to tell anybody just yet that he is the Messiah. Why not? Why would Jesus want the disciples to keep this good news to themselves?

The reason is because, at this point in Matthew's gospel, Jesus' followers do not know what it means for Jesus to be Messiah.

You see, the Jewish people's homeland was occupied by a foreign government. They were policed by Roman troops. It may be an exaggeration to say the Israelites were prisoners in their own land… but that kind of gets to the point.

Since the Jews were God's chosen people, the mindset of some was that God would bring about His kingdom through military force.

We are not immune to this temptation. There are times when I would like to use "force" … and I use that term in its broad sense… to bring folks around to my way of seeing things. But that is not God's way. It does not acknowledge the dignity inherent in others who think differently than I.

So when Jesus tells the disciples that his path involves weakness and vulnerability… postures which will lead to his arrest, humiliation, torture, and execution… his disciples are enraged, even though Jesus says God the Father will raise him from the dead on the third day.

Peter speaks up… once again… and articulates what are likely the feelings of all those around him.

Why can we not overpower all those who oppose us?

Why can we not be the victors?

Why can others not do our bidding?

We have been oppressed for so long. Why can we not feel what it is like to hold the brass ring?

Jesus then calls Peter "Satan" … because what Peter has just said goes against God's will.

Do Jesus' words disturb us in 21st Century America? If they don't, I'm not sure I'm hearing Jesus correctly.

***

We live in the age of the selfie.

There are times we post to social media only the best sides of who we are… we encourage people to look at us and validate what it is we do. And if criticism comes our way, as it does so easily... we segregate our Facebook, Twitter, and Instagram accounts… or whatever the kids are using these days... silence the criticisms, and listen only to the comments which feed our narcissism.

It is easy to idolize the selfie… to be selfish.

It is an involuntary reflex… it is the byproduct of living in the condition of original sin, to think we know better than God how to live our lives.

And, yet, Jesus says: “If any want to become my followers, let them deny themselves and take up their cross and follow me.”

What does it mean for me to deny myself?

***

Asked another way, what motivates hundreds… if not thousands… of volunteers to run in the direction of tragedy instead of away from it, like we have seen this past week with flooding in Texas and Louisiana?

Regardless of whether all of the rescuers are Christian or not, people are denying the temptation to save only themselves… a temptation to which Noah succumbed in the Genesis flood story.

People are instead tapping into the divine indwelling that Jesus calls us to unlock in ourselves.

It is the difference between looking out for number one… and being the keepers of our brothers and sisters.

From a distance, it sounds like an easy choice to make.

But when we think about it, there are voices in American culture which... while cloaking themselves in a Jesus I do not know... promise health and wealth if we simply train ourselves to think positive thoughts.

Because if we think positive thoughts and smile the right way, then we will get those vacant seats on the airplane while others are stuck on standby… we will find a parking spot closest to the grocery store entrance before somebody else does… we will get that promotion at work, leaving co-workers in our wake.

As Stuart Smalley would say, “I’m good enough, I’m smart enough, and doggone it, people like me!”

We may like to eat such philosophical cotton candy from time to time… seems like a good idea at first, but we pay for it later.

That is NOT Christianity. It is a misguided desire to achieve Resurrection without the Cross. It sounds appealing. But it is not based in reality; it is not the way of Jesus.

The way of Jesus is a paradox. And the paradox is that once I admit I am full of selfish tendencies, I can make a conscious choice to ignore them… and once I decide to not let the bad part of me dictate my actions... Christ Jesus can work through me.

God raises me to a new life.

I approach the day not with self-centered arrogance, but self-giving humility.

***

I mentioned a moment ago how we live in the age of the selfie… and I understand how my statement could be heard in a negative light.

We cannot ignore legitimate criticism of a culture in which we are tempted to exaggerate who we are. There is a mindset which says, "look at me."

But let me flip the script a bit. I have noticed this week how the same tools we use to say "look at me" have been turned around to say "look at this."

In flood-stricken areas of Texas and Louisiana, people are using social media to communicate the depth of suffering... and call for help.

The tool of social media has become just that: people communicating with one another for mutual benefit.

It is unfortunate that tragedies have to take place for us to see the good in people, the good in ourselves.

It is unsettling that humanity has to suffer in order for humanity to live into its divine calling.

But that is the paradox communicated by the Cross of Christ which got Peter so upset.

Peter's anger is our anger: why must there be death before resurrection?

Why can God not just come down here and fix things?

The answer is this:

From Scripture we learn that God, in Christ, chooses to use humanity to save humanity.

HUMANITY is created in the image of God… and since we bear God's image, we must claim our divine purpose as we struggle with our weakness… and work with God to bring healing and wholeness to this broken world.

Jesus, Crossfire, and Morton Downey, Jr.

Homily for September 10, 2017

As followers of Jesus, how are we supposed to respond when someone does us wrong? In this morning's gospel passage, Jesus gives us specific instructions on how to resolve conflict. It all seems pretty straight-forward. But do individual Christians, as well as Christian institutions, always follow Jesus' advice?

Conflict sells in our culture. In the 1980s, I remember when a cable TV news channel put on a show called Crossfire … the name itself brings to mind warfare, conflict. At first, the show featured two hosts… one a conservative, political commentator, the other progressive. The set was all dark, ominous, and foreboding... no color or scrolling text across the bottom of the screen like we see today. There was only one thing which demanded our focus: conversation.

But was it really conversation?

The producers of Crossfire would place the show's guest, usually an official from some branch of government, between the opposing hosts. And the hosts would then fire incendiary questions at the government official who was, of course, caught in the crossfire of conflicting world views.

The television industry figured out somewhere along the way that conflict sells. After thirty minutes, or an hour, or however long *Crossfire* lasted, nothing was resolved. The conflict remained.

And Crossfire was the exact kind of show that gave rise to other productions like the Jerry Springer Show… Morton Downey, Jr… Geraldo… Sally Jesse Raphael… and many others. I won't put Oprah in this category because she eventually rose above it.

But when I was in college, several of my friends and I would stay up late at night to watch Morton Downey, Jr… not because we were that interested in the news of the day, but because we wanted to see Mort smoke his cigarette on camera… get in his guests' faces… and yell at them, telling them how stupid they were for thinking the way they did.

Why did America watch these shows? Because we wanted two or more people to get into an argument... and start throwing punches or chairs. We pay to watch persons who are supposed to be adults act like children… that mentality exists in our society.

Think about the structures in our world which thrive on conflict.

Should we accept the narrative that the only way to get ahead in this world is through conflict and not reconciliation?

In Matthew's gospel, Jesus says when another member of the Church sins against us, instead of going directly to that person to find out where the trouble may be, we should go behind that person's back… tell everybody we know how bad that person is… slander them beyond repair… and make ourselves look better in the process.

Actually, that is not what Jesus says. But is that what we do more often than we should?

It is far easier to demonize those with whom we have conflict than to sit down, speak calmly face-to-face, and work to restore balance to a relationship.

Jesus says when another has sinned against us, we should speak with that person privately… talk plainly about what is wrong… and not leave anything unsaid. If the person who has wronged us sees our point of view, great. But if not, we can then bring others with knowledge into the conversation to resolve conflict.

And if that does not work, Jesus says we should then treat our honorable opponent as a Gentile or tax collector.

What does Jesus mean when he tells his first followers, who were Jewish, to treat a sinner as a Gentile or tax collector?

At first read, it may sound like Jesus is saying we can write these people off. Gentiles were not Jews; they were not God's chosen people from the beginning. The mindset was that Gentiles were outsiders… and that led to the notion that those who were not Jewish were beyond God's love.

But if we think back to the gospel lessons we have had from Matthew in recent weeks, we are reminded that Jesus took his followers outside of Jewish territory. We walked with them through Tyre and Sidon, Gentile territory. We remember Jesus' encounter with the Canaanite woman who taught Jesus that God's chosen people are blessed in order to be a blessing to all other peoples. There are no "outsiders" in God's kingdom, only insiders.

Then Matthew gets personal. Matthew writes down words from Jesus which may give us clues to Matthew's own relationship with Jesus: treat the sinner as you would treat a tax collector. Well, Matthew was a tax collector. Matthew was a Jewish man who worked for the Roman government… what an odd position to be in. And it could very well have been that Matthew taxed his fellow Jews more in order to line his own pockets, and not just Caesar's.

So here is Matthew… who traded a life of greed for a life of grace… and Matthew is trying to convey to us how to accept into the fold someone who has done us wrong. Matthew can share this story with integrity because when he wronged others, Jesus loved Matthew into worshiping God and not a government which commodifies its people.

When we consider the conflicts of our day… whether they are at school, at work, in our city, state, nation, or in the world… do we see them as beyond resolution?

Or do we have the guts to take Jesus at his word and endeavor to walk the path of reconciliation… because we realize we are sinners as much as those who sin against us?

The Forgiven Yet Unforgiving Person

Homily for September 17, 2017

I realize it is September 17th… and this is the Fifteenth Sunday after Pentecost. But as we read this morning's passage from Matthew's gospel... and as we again are confronted with news headlines which plant seeds of anxiety in our lives... my mind and spirit are immediately taken to Ash Wednesday… the Church's entry into the penitential season of Lent… a spiritual Spring cleaning, of sorts.

As a side note, the upcoming Ash Wednesday will be on February 14th. What a mixed message that is:

Be my Valentine!

Remember that you are dust!

But I digress.

The message of today's passage from Matthew turns my attention to the Litany of Penitence on page 267 of the Prayer Book… specifically the first petition of this Litany.

The congregation begins with a form of general confession… and the Celebrant then articulates the initial petition, or more accurately, a contrition, which goes like this…

Praying to God: "We have not loved you with our whole heart, and mind, and strength. We have not loved our neighbors as ourselves. We have not forgiven others, as we have been forgiven."

As people of the *Book of Common Prayer*, we will easily recognize the first two sentences. We remember how an expert of the Law (the first five books of the Bible) once asked Jesus to tell him what the most important laws of God were.

Jesus was asked this because some in his day were making the Judaic religion too legalistic… something which can happen in any religion, even today.

There are essentially 613 laws which can be found in the Hebrew tradition… 365 negative commands (thou shalt nots), one for each day of the year…. and 248 positive commands (thou shalt).

People tried to keep these laws, but soon discovered they could not.

We try to do everything right so our lives turn out great, but quickly learn life does not work that way… a revelation which points us to our need of Jesus.

Jesus summarizes the Law by combining verses from Deuteronomy (6:5) and Leviticus (19:18): Love God with all your heart, mind, and strength. Love your neighbor as yourself. We know this.

In the Litany of Penitence on Ash Wednesday, we admit we do not always do what Jesus tells us when it comes to loving both God and neighbor… which leads to the third element to this contrition:

"We have not forgiven others, as we have been forgiven."

This contrition encapsulates the parable Jesus tells this morning… a parable which is as much about predatory lending as it is about recognizing the humanity in those around us.

A king wants to settle accounts with his slaves… one slave cannot pay what he owes, so he begs the king to go easy on him… the slave asks for grace… forgiveness on a loan.

The king shows mercy to the slave.

But when the forgiven slave turns to others who owe him money, this slave does not extend grace, he does not show forgiveness.

Unlike the king, the forgiven slave refused to acknowledge the humanity in the person who owed him money... he saw only dollar signs when those dollars signs were to his benefit… the slave viewed a person indebted to him as a lesser whom he could exploit… this slave took advantage of his privilege… similar to how Pharaoh treated the Hebrews when they were slaves in Egypt.

What happens to the forgiven, yet unforgiving, slave in Jesus' parable is that he is punished by the king in the same way the slave maliciously chose to punish others.

Some might look at this story and get upset with Jesus for saying God will punish humanity in a similar fashion when we act like the slave… and they will cast aspersions on God. But is it fair to blame God in such an instance?

Let us give critical thought to this passage in light of the entire Christian story.

Humanity has a history of placing the blame on God when God does not deserve the blame… and maybe that is why one of the Commandments given to Moses is "don't take the Lord's name in vain" … in other words, do not attribute to God qualities and attributes which do not belong to God… or as it is put in one translation, "You must not use the name of the LORD your God thoughtlessly." (Max Lucado)

In Exodus, some get all bent out of shape when God decides to send the angel of death to kill the firstborn sons of the Egyptians. But when we read the story in its entirety, the punishment imposed on Pharaoh for not letting the Hebrews go is the exact punishment Pharaoh tried to impose on the Hebrews in the first chapter of Exodus. Pharaoh first decreed the genocide of Hebrew boys.

Pharaoh's punishment for himself and his people is the very one he tried to dole out to others.

The Exodus story calls on us to seek perspective and, thus, wisdom.

Today's gospel story implores us to do the same.

Jesus' parable confronts us with the human inclination to take on a victim's mentality while, at the same time, we victimize others.

You see, when Jesus was victimized through his arrest, wrongful conviction, humiliation, and torture, he never played the victim. Instead, Jesus forgave those who did him wrong. "Father, forgive them, for they do not know what they are doing." (Luke 23:24)

Jesus chose not to retaliate… but to instead absorb the worst humanity has to offer and transform it through Cross and Resurrection.

And it is not just the Roman soldiers who were forgiven by Jesus. It was the government of Jesus' day, the religious leaders, the business community… no one group nor one person can be blamed for Jesus' death.

All of humanity was and is responsible for the capital punishment of Jesus.

Even we are complicit in attempting (at times) to silence the voice of God in this world.

So when we realize Jesus forgives us from the Cross and we, thus, benefit daily from God's grace... we are to then extend grace to others in every aspect of our lives.

As followers of Jesus, God's radical call on our lives is to forgive others just as we have been forgiven.

God's Future for St. John's: Fall 2017 Edition

Homily for September 24, 2017

This morning, I am going to reflect on what I hear you telling me about your hopes and dreams for St. John's. I will do this by answering three questions:

Why are we here?

What is God's future for St. John's?

What is your role in God's future for St. John's?

Why are we here?

There is only one reason we are here. We proclaim it each time we speak Eucharistic Prayer A: Christ has died, Christ is Risen, Christ will come again.

That is our story! Jesus of Nazareth, who lived two thousand years ago... was himself God in human flesh... taught us what God's dream for this world is... was wrongly arrested, tortured, and executed… but was raised by the Father on the third day.

Jesus defeated death so that we can live forever with God.

If none of that is true, then we do not need to be here on Sunday mornings.

But if what the Scriptures and the Church say about Jesus IS true… then this story should change not just how we decide to spend every Sunday. It should impact the way we think about each moment of our lives.

Do the decisions I make in life move me closer to God and God's people?

Am I working in my circles of influence to make God's Kingdom on earth a reality?

Each of us is well acquainted with the pain and suffering of the world… and we sense at the deepest part of who we are that there is a better way for humanity to live. We turn to Jesus to show us what that better way is… and we endeavor to make tangible that better way.

We make a conscious choice to bring about God's Kingdom through the life and ministry of St. John's Episcopal Church in Old Town - Saginaw, Michigan.

***

So, what is God's Future for St. John's?

The future of St. John's is, at the core, consistent with our past. We model our faith off the faith of those who were here before us. We are inheritors of this great congregation. God calls us to be faithful stewards in our day, just like those before us, so that there is a St. John's for future generations.

As Episcopalians, we have a particular understanding of Jesus to share with our neighbors… and sharing this understanding is not without risk. We strive to be a big tent, open to "diversity in thought and practice"… a phrase I read recently in a St. John's directory from the 1980s.

Let me read one paragraph from this directory:

"Due to unmanageable repairs and maintenance costs, the ninety-nine-year old rectory was razed in 1978. The other church buildings, maintained by careful stewardship, are in exemplary condition. Lifts have been installed, facilitating entry to the church and offices for persons with physical disabilities. Under the Rev. Chuck Stuart's leadership, the traditional roles for church women have been expanded into all areas of church work, including the priesthood…"

As I read this, I see three things:

St. John's has a history of making needed decisions, even when those decisions are difficult.

St. John's has a history of properly caring for its buildings.

St. John's has a history of bringing into the FULL life and ministry of the Church persons who were once (and are sometimes still, increasingly so) marginalized.

This is who St. John's has been. This is who St. John's is today. This is who we hope to be in the future.

***

So, what is YOUR role in God's future for St. John's?

When I arrived here in late December, early January… you began to tell me about two projects which needed to be done, projects long talked about, but not yet acted on.

The first is the construction of a columbarium, a structure inside the church with niches for urns which contain the cremated remains of the dead. You have achieved your objective.

The columbarium is on-site… the chapel (now called Calvary Chapel) will soon receive new paint and carpet… we will consecrate the columbarium on November 5th. This is, for all intents and purposes, DONE. You have accomplished one of your goals.

The second task is repairing some of the stained-glass windows. The most recent cost estimate is around $150,000. A committee is being formed to work out the proper mixture of fund-raising, loans, endowment leveraging, and crowd-sourcing to get this project started soon.

The idea is to receive pledges and dollars for window restoration over the course of the next three or four years.

As the money comes in and the work is done between now and about 2022, we in the St. John's community will spend time prayerfully and systematically developing a Strategic Plan.

We will sharpen our focus with mission and ministry.

We will determine how to update and further beautify the education wing, the community room, as well as some facets of the Nave and Sanctuary... both internally and externally.

We will be faithful in our day to position future generations of St. John's for a deeper, stronger witness of Jesus Christ.

We will do for future members of St. John's what previous members have done for us.

***

So, what does the St. John's community require of me? And what does the St. John's community require of you?

Each of us needs to pray about how God can work fully in us. God will not call you to invest yourself the way that God calls another to invest. God is not in the business of playing favorites. But God will call you to do what it is God has created you to do.

I ask you to pray about how God might use you to solidify St. John's for both the present and future.

***

We are coming off the summer months, so our financial giving for 2017 needs to catch up to an already ambitious budget. Income is not yet in line with where it needs to be for this time of year. Each of us needs to be attentive to that now so we do not have a big gap in December.

At the same time, I ask you to pray about your giving of time, talent, and treasure to St. John's as we formulate plans to be God's Church in the 21st Century and beyond.

I firmly believe God needs St. John's and the Episcopal Church in these peculiar times.

May we have the grace to pray fervently about how God might work through each and all of us… and, then, let us have some fun getting the job done.

OCTOBER

Thinking for Myself about Jesus

Homily for October 1, 2017

This morning we again stumble across a passage from Matthew's Gospel which makes no sense unless we first learn what comes before it. Jesus is teaching in the synagogue, no doubt talking about the Kingdom of Heaven, what God intends for humanity. And Jesus is interrupted by members of the religious establishment: some chief priests and elders.

These are the stalwarts of the religious community in Jesus' day. People turned to them for a word from God when needed. They were well-respected. They were trusted. And so, we have to wonder: why are these religious leaders so upset with Jesus?

When we look at the paragraphs leading up to the first verse we encounter this morning, we learn that Jesus took radical actions which set the political, economic, and religious establishments on edge:

Jesus entered Jerusalem on a donkey and colt… he overturned the tables of the money changers in the temple… and he cursed a fig tree.

We recognize these events from our liturgical observance of Holy Week. On the day we call Palm Sunday, Jesus entered Jerusalem riding on a donkey and a colt. Scholars tell us that around the same time, Pontius Pilate… then the Roman governor of the area… entered Jerusalem on a horse.

The horse is symbolic of war. The donkey and colt are symbolic of peace. Jesus visually challenged the corrupt political system of his day.

Taking it a step further, Jesus went to the temple in Jerusalem where the faithful came to offer sacrifices to God. In order for the faithful to make an offering to God, they needed to buy animals to sacrifice. This became a big racket. The establishment made profits on peoples' devotion to God.

Those who worship the almighty dollar put themselves in a position to prey… p-r-E-y… on those who worship the Almighty God. And Jesus tells them: quit it! Do not do it!

Thirdly, Jesus cursed a fig tree.

Speech can bless... and speech can curse.

Remember how God SPOKE creation into being… how Jesus SPOKE into the tomb, and Lazarus walked out alive.

What do we do with our speech? When do we bless, and when do we curse?

The fig tree is symbolic of God's people who were supposed to bear fruit and speak God's blessing to all of humanity. And when they... similar to how the Church has done from time to time... failed to speak properly for God, Jesus spoke against them for getting off track. Jesus cursed the fig tree… and the fig tree withered.

So, in just a few paragraphs, Jesus upsets the political, economic, and religious establishments… and that is why some chief priests and elders interrupt his teaching in the synagogue. They ask him: Who do you think you are? What gives you the authority to usurp our authority?

Jesus answers their questions by asking a question, a technique Jesus uses often. When we question a questioner, we find out the motives which undergird the questions.

Jesus asks those who have interrupted his teaching a question about John the Baptist. John the Baptist was an extremely popular, anti-establishment religious figure of the day… who boldly proclaimed that Jesus was the long-awaited Messiah of God.

How the chief priests and elders answer the question about John the Baptist will logically determine what they should think about Jesus. And the question is: "Did the baptism of John come from heaven, or was it of human origin?" And remember: the baptism of John included the call on people to repent of their sins… stop going their own way, start going God's way.

Let us follow the thinking of the chief priests and elders as they consider how to answer Jesus.

They begin to argue with each other to determine their response... and they find themselves in a bind. They realize that if they decide to say the baptism of John came from heaven (if John the Baptist is a prophet of God), then the chief priests and elders would have to believe John's message that Jesus is the Messiah. And they clearly do not… or, at least, they do not want to.

If they choose to say John's ministry has nothing to do with God, then because of John's popularity, they would alienate themselves from the very people they are supposed to represent and embrace.

Do you see their problem? The chief priests and elders are asking, and now answering, questions about Jesus and truth. But they really do not want to accept the truth about Jesus… because accepting the truth about Jesus means they would have to change how they see themselves and the world around them.

The chief priests and elders make a conscious choice to be more concerned with how their answer will be interpreted by those around them. They are anxious about maintaining their popularity and standing in the community.

In an effort to cover themselves, their answer to Jesus is a cop out: we do not know. We know if the baptism of John was from heaven or of mere human origin. They are not willing to think critically about what it is that Jesus has been doing. They are afraid of giving an answer that might be unpopular with those they answer to… either up the food chain, or among the constituency they supposedly represent.

And because they will not answer Jesus… Jesus logically cannot answer them.

Jesus cannot provide an answer because the chief priests and elders are so wrapped up in their own egos that they are incapable of listening to the Voice of God in their midst.

The religious establishment had a preconceived notion of God… and that preconceived notion of God (dare I say "idol") gave the chief priests and elders their identity… so, changing the way they thought about God meant changing their understanding of themselves. And that is a hard thing to do… even when they experienced God, first hand, in a potentially life-giving way.

Who is God, if God is not who I thought?

What is life, if I have been looking at God the wrong way?

Who am I, if I have built my identity on a false understanding of God?

Now, I do not want to be overly critical of the chief priests and elders and their stubborn mindset... because if I were, I would be overly critical of myself. On more than one occasion, there is nothing the Spirit of Christ could tell me… because I would hold on for dear life to what I now see as a limited understanding of God, the world, and myself.

I wonder, though, if Matthew had written a sequel to his Gospel if we would have found out how this encounter with Jesus might have changed the minds of these particular chief priests and elders.

How might these religious leaders have been transformed once they stopped caring about the fleeting opinions of others… and began to use their God-given hearts and intellects to decide for themselves about Jesus?

How might we be different if we die to the need for the approval of others… consider the truth about Jesus on its own merit… and then allow Jesus to direct us in the way we should go?

What Christians Can Do with Their Thoughts and Prayers

Homily for October 8, 2017

Just about every Monday morning of the year, I begin the process of writing a sermon for the following Sunday. The process should include thoughtful and prayerful study of the upcoming Bible lessons… reflection on my conversations with many of you from recent days, weeks, and now months… and a glance at the news to see what is going on in our world.

In recent years, preachers have been called on increasingly to bring understanding to events which are often labeled "senseless."

From a pulpit, it is one thing to speak about pain and suffering, as well as humanity's responsibility to one another, in the aftermath of natural disasters.

I think "sobering nuance" is called for when preachers consider what to say in the wake of violence.

We had yet another mass shooting in America this past week. Our nation is again debating, in a divisive way, how "we the people" should respond.

We at St. John's are not immune to the temptation of divisive debate… which is precisely why the Church should work to model civil discourse.

In speaking with many of you, I know that in the St. John's family we start from different places when it comes to potential solutions for the problems we face as Americans.

And that is okay.

I believe we can leverage our diversity to bring about blessings which unite.

Because the role of the Church is not the same as that of government… my job as your priest is to dig deep into the Scriptures and address what gives rise to the challenges we are called to tackle in our society.

I trust the Holy Spirit to empower you, the laity of the Church, to turn our "thoughts and prayers" into godly actions… to faithfully accomplish in our communities what we say at the end of each Sunday Mass: "Go in peace to love and serve the Lord."

In this morning's passage from Matthew's Gospel... and considering its logical extension... I see two things which are relevant to how we engage our society Monday through Saturday:

1) Humanity too often resorts to violence to overcome difference
2) The God we meet in Jesus Christ emboldens humanity to stop the cycle of violence

Jesus tells the parable of a "landowner" who plants a vineyard... builds a wall around it… puts a wine press inside... and constructs a watchtower for security.

The "landowner" LEASES the vineyard to a group of "tenants" … the job of the tenants is to cultivate wine.... and when we consider how wine is understood in several parts of the Scriptures, we might say the job of the tenants is to cultivate joy and gladness. From our Isaiah reading, we learn the fruit of the tenants should be justice and righteousness.

The "landowner" goes away. A distance is created between the landowner and tenants.

There comes a time when the landowner wants to collect from the vineyard the fruit he desires; the landowner wishes to receive from the tenants joy and gladness, justice and righteousness. But what happens in the time of distance is that the tenants decide they want to control the vineyard.

They are no longer content to cultivate joy and gladness on the landowner's terms.

The tenants seek autonomy with respect to the land, their livelihood, and their security... and, when separated from the landowner, they cultivate violence.

Now, on one level, Jesus speaks here about God's relationship with a particular group of people… and how a religious establishment dealt with critical voices, and would eventually deal with him.

But I think this story operates on multiple levels.

The landowner sends a series of emissaries, ambassadors to collect what is rightfully his. But those persons are met with violence at the hands of the tenants; some are killed.

The landowner then sends his son, thinking the tenants would respect the son.

But the tenants kill the son, as well, arrogantly surmising this act of violence will achieve the desired result.

This mindset exists today.

We want to be in control… we do not want anyone else to control us… and we are sometimes tempted to use any means necessary to gain and retain control.

But the temptation to ultimate control is a lie.

In the grand scheme of God's vineyard, only God can be in control… and when we come to understand this in its proper context, we see how the terms of God's lease give life.

One of the things I find concerning in Jesus' parable is that the landowner… who is symbolic of God… leaves the vineyard for a distant country.

When I take the Christian story as a whole… and consider the different names for God in the Hebrew Scriptures... I KNOW God is always with us.

Yes, God can seem distant at times. But I know God is always close, even when it does not feel like it.

If I allow myself to feel like God is not close, my mind can go down all sorts of rabbit trails.

When I feel like God is not close… then God must not love me… and to think I am unloved, or worse yet unlovable, is heartbreaking… so out of pain and vulnerability I try to take control of my life.

With this self-produced anxiety, I lash out at others who threaten me simply by their existence.

One truth of the human condition is that we can convince ourselves, wrongly, that God's love is in short supply… and when we do that, we diminish the humanity of others in order to elevate our own.

When humanity resorts to violence, it hurts not only those toward whom violence is directed.

As Jesus' parable contends, it eventually backfires on those committing the violence.

We have heard it before, and it bears repeating: hurt people hurt people.

But with critical thought and fervent prayer, we discover that God's love has no limits.

God loves ALL at the expense of NONE.

This truth both COMFORTS and TRANSFORMS me when my "thoughts and prayers" are centered on the Cross of Christ.

This truth is what I believe should serve as the foundation for solving the problems of the world.

Jesus shows us how to take the pain we experience in this life… and NOT allow the pain inflicted on us… to be motivation… to inflict pain on others.

May God grant us wisdom to recognize humanity's temptation to evil and capacity for good… courage to stop the cycle of violence… and resolve in our corner of the vineyard to cultivate joy, gladness, justice, righteousness, and peace.

You Are Missed

Homily for October 15, 2017

This past week, I attended a gathering of the All Michigan Episcopal Network… on Mackinac Island… at the Grand Hotel. Yes, I stayed at the Grand Hotel… at a sharply decreased nightly rate.

Eight weeks before the conference, I and other Episcopal clergy were e-mailed an outline... which included how to get to the island, a schedule of events, and whatnot. Seven and a half weeks after that e-mail showed up in my inbox, I decided to read it. And that is a good thing.

Did you know that to have dinner at the Grand Hotel you must dress in formal attire? I do not have any formal attire. I have a bunch of black clothes and white dog collars… which I promptly took to the dry cleaners.

I had to wake up to what that e-mail was telling me… and attend to my clothing options to the best of my ability. After all, it was the Grand Hotel. And you know what? It worked out. I had a grand time dining and conversing with people, some I already knew… and I met some new friends, as well. It was quite the banquet.

***

In this morning's gospel lesson, Jesus again tries to explain the Kingdom of Heaven.

Remember: Heaven is not something we experience ONLY after we die… we can have heaven RIGHT NOW.

Jesus compares the Kingdom of Heaven to a wedding banquet a parent throws for a child.

You know this, because I have been with you for a few weddings already. YOU know how to party at weddings… and it is not just the dining and the dancing, it is the conversations around tables and in speeches which tap into the deepest of our emotions.

In Jesus' story, the king first invites to the wedding banquet a select group of people… but nobody wants to go. In their minds, they had more important things to do. Some preferred to spend time outdoors, others wanted to get more work done at the office. I am not making this up. It is in the text.

Now, Jesus uses hyperbole to make a point. The punchline is that those who make no time for the king and the son logically do not enjoy the wedding banquet.

So, when the king in the parable lashes out at the party poopers… we should NOT understand that God will retaliate against humanity when we "make light" of God's invitation.

No, God loves us so much that God allows us to accept or reject the Divine invitation... and when we choose to reject, the natural consequence is that we close ourselves off from God.

The king goes back to the drawing board and sends out invitations for others. He wants the wedding hall full of guests. And the king gets his wish.

But when the king arrives at the banquet, he notices a guest not wearing the proper wedding attire. And what happens to this guest is probably what would have happened to me had I shown up to the Grand Hotel without nice clothes.

This particular guest is supposed to take personal initiative when attending the king's banquet; he has to put on the robe the king provides for all the guests. But this guest refuses… and that leads to his exit.

***

I think you know me well enough by now to know that what I am about to say I do not say while pointing the bony finger of shame. I love you guys.

But there are stark truths in this parable we cannot avoid.

God is non-stop inviting us to the Heavenly Banquet… we are summoned over, and over, and over, and over again.

But we have to RSVP to God's invitation. We need to show up. And, yes, I am talking about church attendance… but we also need to be proactive about recognizing God's presence in our lives Monday through Saturday.

In the language of the parable, we need to put on the proper wedding garment. As important as it is to show up… there is so much more to the Christian life than that… we need to allow the God we know in Jesus to blanket us in love.

If we do not get this, we miss out on the depth of relationship we can have with God and each other right now… and we will fail to see the importance of inviting into the Episcopal Church people who are turned away from so many other banquets.

***

When I was in college... and home for the weekend or summer... I refused to go to church; I did not take an active role in my faith.

Each Sunday when my parents got home from church, my mother would walk through the door and say: "They missed you."

They missed me?

No, they did not miss me! They did not even know me. How could they know me when I chose not to show up?

If you miss someone, it is because you have a deep bond with them… and with deep bonds, people can celebrate with each other in good times… and support one another when life throws a curveball.

And since I had no deep bonds with people from that church... then, no, nobody missed me.

Well, nobody except God.

***

I do not remember how long it took for me to get over myself and understand what my mother was really saying.

But I got back into church… not the Episcopal Church my parents attended… but the banquet hall God was preparing for me all along… and had I not responded to God's invitation, I shudder to think how difficult and lonely the next years of my life would have been.

Given all the blessings I received, and still receive, following that one decision… independent of my call to the priesthood... It is hard for me to imagine where I would be now without God and the people of the Episcopal Church.

This is what I want for you… and this is what I want for people who are not yet engaged in the St. John's community, but probably need to be. I am thinking you know of at least one person who could benefit from being part of the St. John's family.

I want you and others to encounter and enjoy the depth of the banquet God throws for us all in Christ Jesus.

I can tell you about God's invitation… and I will do that over and over. But I cannot accept it for you.

You have to do that yourself.

And when you do, I bet my life you will be blessed beyond your current imagination.

This is (Not) Us

Homily for October 22, 2017

One late afternoon not too long ago, I was here at the church getting ready to go home. The phone rang. It was not a telephone call. It was somebody at the door.

If you have ever spent any time in the St. John's office, you know the phone has a different ring when somebody hits the button at the door. We pick up the receiver… people at the door can talk to us… we hit a button on the phone, and it unlocks the door.

At least, that is what I am told. I do not know how to work this new-fangled technology. So, I just walked down here and opened the door myself.

Now, there was a woman at the door I had not met before. She said she had something to return to the church.

The woman handed me a photograph. She said she had purchased the picture at an auction and thought somebody at St. John's might like to have it.

She said it was a picture of St. John's.

I thanked her. She went on her way.

I didn't have the heart to tell the woman. The picture she gave to me certainly is a picture of a church. But it is not a picture of St. John's Episcopal Church in Old Town Saginaw, Michigan.

It is the image of a different church in town. There are striking similarities. I understand how this person mistook the church in the picture for St. John's... and she was very sweet to bring the picture. But it was not St. John's.

This makes me wonder: when people think of St. John's... what image comes to their minds?

***

In this morning's Gospel lesson, a group of Pharisees attempts to trap Jesus in his words.

Pharisees were members of the religious establishment in Jesus' day. At the risk of over-simplification, their job was to make sure all the rules and regulations of God were kept.

They were well-meaning, if not a bit threatened by Jesus.

And that is why some of them are trying to set a trap for Jesus. They ask Jesus whether it is appropriate for the Jewish people to pay taxes to the Roman emperor.

Remember, the Roman Empire occupied the Jewish homeland in Jesus' time. The Jews did not have self-rule... they were searching for someone to liberate them. And in their search, they ask Jesus the question:

Should the Jews pay taxes to the Roman empire?

Here is why this question is a trap. If Jesus says it is not appropriate to pay taxes to Rome, then he could be accused of treason. He would be speaking out against the government.

If Jesus says it IS lawful for Jews to pay taxes to Rome, then he would have sold out to the culture... more loyal to Rome than to the God of Israel.

Jesus is not fooled by what is going on. He asks for a coin used to pay taxes… and then asks the Pharisees to tell him whose image is on the coin.

Stay with me. This is an important question. Whose image is on the coin?

Of course, the image of the Roman emperor was on the coin shown to Jesus… much like we have Lincoln on a penny, Jefferson on a nickel, Roosevelt on a dime, Washington on a quarter, and Kennedy on a half-dollar.

Jesus then says: "Give to the emperor the things that are the emperor's, and to God the things that are God's."

Do you see what is happening here?

Jesus changes the conversation. We are not talking about taxes anymore. Yes, we could glean from Jesus that it is appropriate to pay taxes.

But look deeper… and this is something I learned from Christian apologist Ravi Zacharias.

The items stamped with the image of the Roman emperor are to be given back to the Roman emperor. This is what Jesus says.

But Jesus says something else not elaborated on by Matthew, which means we need to use our God-given intellects to understand what Jesus is saying. We cannot just move on to the next paragraph.

Jesus says we are to give to God the things that are God's.

That which is crafted in God's image must return to God.

Are you with me?

In the book of Genesis (1:27) we read:

God created humankind in his image, in the image of God he created them; male and female he created them.

You, I, and everybody we meet are created in the image of God. Jesus says we are to return each image of God to God. We are to return ourselves to God. Our lives are to reflect the character of God, which we see in Jesus.

All of humanity is created in the image of God. But when we look at what is going on in the world… it is clear this is not a universally held belief.

Some groups of people created in the image of God are still considered subhuman… other thans… lesser than how God has created ME and US (whoever "I" am, whoever "WE" are).

Like the Roman emperor, there are literal and metaphorical ways in which the "in crowd" stamps its image… and will accept in return only the items which reflect the image of the "in crowd."

And if we are going to be honest about all of this, the Institutional Church needs to acknowledge and repent of its share of the blame when it comes to the dehumanization of persons created in God's image.

Now here's the good news. As I thought to myself when I saw a picture of the other church: This is not us.

This is not St. John's Episcopal Church in Old Town Saginaw, Michigan.

If this is not us, then who are we?

What image are we called to on God and others we encounter?

As followers of Jesus, we give to God all who are stamped in God's image… which is far more difficult than it sounds.

Not everybody we meet in this life believes they are created in God's image… because in so many ways, they are told they are not.

Part of who we are as Episcopal Christians means we have the temerity to believe God's love for humanity has no limits.

As our new bishop, Catherine Waynick, said yesterday at diocesan convention: "God loves you, and there is nothing you can do to change that."

So when we meet people who have been turned away by those claiming to act in the name of God, as well meaning as those persons are... and as much as those people, themselves, are loved by God… it is our calling to reflect the love of Jesus onto the marginalized… and invite them into this community, so they can come to know the love of God we encounter in Jesus.

God's Future for St. John's Stained Glass Windows

Homily for October 29, 2017

Last Sunday during the announcement time I mentioned what I would speak about from the pulpit this morning. And it is this: We are moving ahead with the restoration of the stained glass windows.

In a few moments, I will share the math done by treasurer Burris Smith which shows just how doable this project is. But why should we invest in the restoration of stain glass windows? In my mind, this is easy.

We have a story to tell. In the person of Jesus of Nazareth, we learn that the God who created all there is loves us beyond our wildest imagination. The Risen Christ transforms and empowers individuals, communities, and societies.

Those who came before us at 123 N. Michigan Avenue thought enough of us to tell this story, even though they never met any or most of us. I believe we are called by God to take into consideration people who are not yet here, people not yet born, people whom God already knows, and do our part in our day to (in the words of the Apostle Paul) pass along as of first importance what we received: *"... that Christ died for our sins in accordance with the scriptures,*[4] *and that he was buried, and that he was raised on the third day in accordance with the scriptures..."* (1 Corinthians 15:3-4)

We say it every week: Christ has died. Christ is Risen. Christ will come again. That is what we received. That is what we proclaim today. That is what we are to pass on.

As Episcopal Christians, we tell this story not with words only. But with liturgy, music, art, architecture, and so much more. Yes, we have a historic building to take care of, but St. John's is not a museum in which we are mere curators of beautiful things which no longer have any practical use. No, we are a living, dynamic, Holy Spirit-charged outpost of the Jesus Movement, and we cannot deny the sacramental power of this physical structure to impact lives for the better.

These stained glass windows help us proclaim that Jesus is Lord. That is why we are moving ahead with this project. Here's how we are going to do it.

Recently, I mentioned from the pulpit a cost estimate from a couple of years ago which was in the neighborhood of $150,000, and that was just for the center sections of the windows at the front and back of the church. What I should have done (I ask your forgiveness for not doing so) was mention the estimate which includes all of the windows at the front and back of the church.

That estimate in 2015 was $190,000. Today it is $203,000.

We are not yet talking about the side window because it is the center windows which need our immediate attention.

Over the past several years, there have been contributions to the stained-glass windows fund. We have roughly $14,000 for the windows already. In recent weeks, we received a pledge (anonymously) of $50,000 toward window restoration. There are grants we will apply for, and there are others who are expressing interest in giving to this project. I give thanks to God for these people and their willingness to step forward.

But we will not accomplish our goal through one person or three or five, and it would be unhealthy for St. John's to rely on a few to support the whole. For a Christian community to maximize its effectiveness, each person within the community must answer God's call. It is going to take God working through all of us to get this windows project done.

As an aside, when we talk about giving to the windows project, this is in addition to what we currently give toward keeping the lights on and paying salaries, doing outreach, and whatnot. At a forum on November 12th, we will talk about the annual budget as well as a capital campaign a few years from now to address needed updates to the entire campus. We have a lot of God's work to do, and I could not be more excited.

For now, consider the math done by our Treasurer, Burris Smith. If we consider the $203,000 estimate, the $14,000 already in the bank, and the $50,000 pledge, what is left is $139,000 to be raised among the St. John's family.

Our plan is to do this over the course of three years. We have 156 individuals or families who currently offer financial support to St. John's. For this group of 156 to make up $139,000 over the course of the next three years, that means each individual or family who contributes to St. John's would need to increase their giving each week by six dollars.

Can you give six more dollars to St. John's each Sunday for the next three years?

I will, with God's help.

Just so that you are aware, as your rector, I do not look at individual giving records. I do not know how much money any of you gives to St. John's, unless you tell me. But I do not need to know. And I do not want to know. That is between you and God.

I realize it is somewhat of a risk to speak about parish finances in general terms because each of us is in a different place economically. And that is fine. But I hope you see my point: we can do this when we pull together, when we each pray and act individually, when we all pray and act together as a parish family.

As for me and my family, we are all in. I ask you to pray about your participation, as we prepare the windows for the next century of mission and ministry in Old Town. There are plenty in our community who need to hear the message of God's love in Jesus, and there are many who need to hear it in the various ways we at St. John's proclaim it.

NOVEMBER

God the Knitter

Homily for November 5, 2017
All Saints' Day - Transferred

(At the 10:30am service) In a few moments, we as the family of St. John's will bless our new columbarium in Calvary Chapel. A columbarium is a structure in which the ashes of departed persons are placed until Christ Jesus returns to make all of Creation new.

This project was planted in our hearts by God many years ago… much hoped for in moments of doubt… and it has now come to fruition.

God's timing could not be better.

This weekend, Christians around the world commemorate the Feast of All Saints, which falls on November 1st… but we have moved the observance to today.

We began this liturgy with elements from the feast of All Faithful Departed, from November 2nd. And that included our prayers for members of the St. John's family who died in the past year.

A crude, if not cynical, way of distinguishing All Saints from All Faithful Departed is that All Saints is for remembering people like Mother Teresa… while All Faithful Departed (or All Souls) is for people like me.

But when we attempt to elevate some followers of Jesus over others, we miss the larger point of this observance.

The point is found in the Collect of the Day: "Almighty God, you have knit together your elect in one communion and fellowship in the mystical body of your Son Christ our Lord…"

Whom does God knit together in Christ?

The collect invites us to imagine God with knitting needles and yarn… executing in perfect fashion a spiritual garter stitch, moss stitch, purl, or selvage. I have no idea what any of those terms are… other than (I am told) they have something to do with knitting.

To me, knitting is a mystery.

God's knitting together of the living and the dead in Christ, through the power of the Holy Spirit is a mystery, as well… yet that is why we are here. We gather to remember that we are still bonded… we are still joined… we are still knitted together with all of our loved ones who have died, those now in God's direct presence.

This is what we mean when we talk about the Communion of Saints… the connection we reference each time we celebrate Holy Communion.

For me, today is one of those days when I choke up from both sadness and joy… holding each of these emotions at the same time without diminishing either.

As we walk with Christ Jesus, we are mindful of the range of emotions brought to the surface by All Saints and All Faithful Departed… sadness on one end of the spectrum, joy on the other… and everything else in between.

It is a struggle to ride the rollercoaster of sadness and joy… wondering how much time to give to the pain of our past without being consumed by it... or to a future joy at the risk of it becoming an escape from reality… all the while making sure the pain and joy we locate in our past and future do not distract us from God's gift of the present.

What we should keep in mind is this:

As we observe the feasts of All Saints and All Faithful Departed, Christian "tradition and ritual" makes space for us to grieve in healthy ways the deaths of those we love…we are offered sound reason to hope for God's future… and in Christ, through the power of the Holy Spirit, we are motivated to embrace, and not waste, God's life for us right now.

Thy Kingdom Come

Homily for November 12, 2017

I have been thinking a lot this week about a particular phrase in the prayer Jesus taught his followers. In King James language, it is this: "... thy Kingdom come, thy will be done on earth, as it is in heaven."

Each time we recite the Lord's prayer, we demand (we do not ask), we demand that God's dream for the human race become a reality.

I wonder if we pray this prayer so often that we forget how radical it is.

The choir gave voice last week to Revelation 21, a musical expression of the hope deeply embedded in the soul of humanity… lyrics which point to God's dream for us.

What we demand NOW is for God to dwell with us… for us to be God's people… and through this intimate relationship, God "... will wipe away every tear from (our) eyes. Death will be no more; mourning and crying and pain will be no more, for the first things will have passed away." (Revelation 21:3-4)

Holy Scripture paints for us a picture of a time and place where there are no tears, no death, no mourning, crying, or pain. The task of those who endeavor to follow Jesus is to frame this picture… and display it in the gallery of the world.

While many of our nation's leaders are stuck in neutral following yet another episode of mass violence, we in the Church will point to the God revealed in Jesus, present in the Holy Spirit, and proclaim: here is the direction we need to go!

No tears. No death. No mourning. No crying. No pain.

This is God's ideal we are to demand… AND work toward.

It is not some mirage humanity is vainly crawling for in our desert of suffering.

It is too often the case that we lament a tragedy with one group of victims… only to learn of a new crisis... and turn our attentions to the newest victims, just like the national news networks.

Rinse and repeat.

We as a nation... an often passive, viewing public... have not yet made the right choices to break this cycle.

We are slaves to "tragedy fatigue" and "competitive victimhood" (Rabbi Jonathan Sacks)… too jaded, indecisive, or beholden to a partisan ideology to bring tangible and lasting change.

This is where God desires to enter the picture.

In this morning's Gospel passage, Jesus again tries to explain what life can be like when God is at the center of our lives: 24/7/365. The punchline to the parable is this:

The Kingdom of Heaven is coming.

God is trying to enter our lives.

There is a better way for us to live as a society.

We need to be on the lookout for God's Kingdom… which means we need to be awake… we need to have, as Jesus says, oil in our lamps… fuel to keep lighting the way to God's future.

***

Contrary to what some popular TV preachers like to say, God has not withdrawn from America because of particular sins; God has not removed the proverbial "hedge of protection" from around this nation.

If God has removed a hedge, it is not to let evil in… it is to tear down the hedge we plant to shield ourselves from God.

Humanity often places a barrier between ourselves and God because we prefer to be in control.

Yes, we say we want God… but what we mean is we want God as we choose to define God, and we want this God on our own terms.

But what happens when we accept God on God's terms?

With God on God's terms, we begin to see the necessity and benefit of community over individualism.

With God on God's terms, the truth of the Baptismal Covenant transforms our hearts… we hear in a different way the phrase "... respect the dignity of every human being."

With God on God's terms, we dispel the self-destructive notion that the world should revolve around me and people of my kind... and all others should cater to my every whim and want.

In our culture, we are told over and over again our primary concern should be to watch out for number one.

Pay no attention to THY will be done… clear the way for MY will to be done.

***

But as Dr. Phil says, "How is that working out for us?"

How is that working for us?

It is not working.

We cannot keep going like this… and we all know it.

The Christian Church says… our only help is in the Name of the Lord, the Maker of Heaven and Earth (Psalm 121).

Now is the time to allow God to draw closer.

Now is the time to put ourselves in a position to listen for how God desires to work through us to make God's dream for this world a reality.

On the individual level, maybe this means making the extra effort to be with this beloved community on Sundays more often…

Or deepening our "prayer life" and "service to our community" Monday through Saturday...

Or finally saying "yes" to God's call… that internal tug we work so hard to ignore.

Is God calling you to be a deacon or priest in the Episcopal Church?

Is God calling you to a more focused ministry as a lay person?

For everybody in this room, the answer to one of those questions is "yes."

***

There are many problems in our world today, and government cannot solve them alone… if government can solve them at all.

We need to disabuse ourselves of the idea that the Church's time to engage and influence the culture has passed... and that Christians should just keep to ourselves and leave society's challenges to secular, non-theistic entities.

Nothing could be further from the truth.

The Church's time is now.

May the God we know in Christ... work through us… a beloved community empowered by the Holy Spirit… so that God's will is done on earth as it is in heaven.

God Language

Homily for November 19, 2017

One of the beautiful things about moving to Michigan is I am learning a new language.

For example, the word "M-A-C-K-I-N-A-C" is pronounced Mackinaw. Not to be confused with "M-A-C-K-I-N-A-W" which is pronounced Mackinaw.

One of our neighboring communities is spelled "B-U-E-N-A" Vista. How that is pronounced "Byoona" Vista and not "Buena" Vista I will never know. Maybe it is somehow associated with "Yoopers," as in the U-P… the Upper Peninsula. To me, I thought the U-P was a soap opera on Fox. Or maybe that was the O-C.

If we are talking about Coke, or Sprite, or Verner's, it is not soda. It's pop.

When we say Garber, or Draper, or Serra, we are talking about car dealerships. Honestly, I have never seen so many car dealers per capita as I have here. Not that there is anything wrong with that.

It stands to reason that language brings association. And at times, a term used in one context can mean something completely different in a separate context.

The restaurant Fuzzy's in Saginaw is an American diner which serves a Cowboy Burger.

The restaurant Fuzzy's in Texas serves Mexican food to Cowboys.

***

So when we use the word GOD… what associations do we make?

In this morning's Gospel lesson, Jesus tells a parable which prompts us to consider how we think about God. Jesus tells this story using the language of a "man" who entrusts property to his "slaves"... language many find troublesome in the 21st Century, but we need to move past it for the moment.

Each slave is given a different amount of currency to invest while the man goes on a journey.

Two of the slaves make good investments with the currency given to them by the man. But it is the third slave who is the focus of this parable. This third slave takes the money his master has given him, digs a hole in the ground, and hides it.

He does nothing with the gift given to him.

When the man returns from his journey to collect on his investment, he is pleased with what he receives from the first two slaves. But listen to what the third slave says to the man when he has to explain himself.

The third slave says: "I knew that you were a harsh man… so I was afraid… and I hid what you gave me."

Since the "man" in this story represents God and the "slaves" are symbolic of humanity… Jesus points us to a popular conception about God which is false.

Jesus is showing us that the way we see God impacts how we live our lives.

If we believe God is harsh, angry, and out to punish us if we do wrong… then we will live our lives in fear… we will "hide" the gift of life that God has given us… and we will shy away from the prophetic call to do justice, love kindness, and walk humbly with our God. (Micah 6:8)

When I read this parable, it is tempting to want to throw "other" Christian denominations under the bus… criticizing them for having too small a view of God… not being as loving as I think they should be.

The truth of the matter is it is too often the case that I am the "third slave" in Jesus' parable. I am tempted to move through life out of the fear that I am going to be punished by God for investing Divine currency in the wrong way.

***

This afternoon at 4pm, the St. John's family will host an interfaith Thanksgiving service. In this building will be a gathering of Jews, Muslims, Buddhists, Hindus, Baha'is, Jainists, Catholics, Mormons, and Methodists.

I think you know me well enough by now to understand that I have a very deep love for my Savior and Lord, Christ Jesus. I hold my view of Christ with conviction… and because of my understanding of Christ, I carry around with me a great deal of humility.

Conviction and humility all rolled into one.

As this day approached, and in spite of the fact I have made some really good, new friends as we have planned this service, I have become very aware of my fears.

What will other Christians think of me for worshiping next to non-Christians… and especially Muslims, who are frequently targeted unfairly in our current climate?

Will I be seen as less of a Christian?

Could I be labeled a heretic?

I shared this concern with our new bishop, Catherine Waynick, in hopes there would be no Episcopal retribution against your rector. What she said to me about hosting an interfaith service is this:

"We should do together as much as we can."

We should do together as much as we can.

Bishop Waynick's response to my concern is life-giving. It gets to the depth of God's love which is communicated in Jesus' parable.

When we live our lives thinking God is harsh, making our stance toward God rooted in fear, then we shortchange ourselves.

But when we come to see in Jesus how God's love is boundless… we can use this Divine currency to make our lives rich.

Christian Authority

Homily for November 26, 2017

Today, Christians around the world commemorate what has come to be known as "Christ the King" Sunday. The older I get, and the more I learn about Jesus, the more I am baffled… if not troubled... by this designation.

What does the Church mean when she says Christ is King?

I am not convinced the royal moniker translates in our culture.

On July 29, 1981, I remember waking up early with my mother, brother, and sister to watch the royal wedding of Diana and Charles. While that marriage would not make it through the 90s, Americans were captivated by English pomp and circumstance… the fairy-tale ceremony which fed and fueled our mythological understanding of royalty.

In retrospect, a cynic might say it all pointed to a people of privilege, placed on a pedestal by commoners of lesser lineage, catered to by the masses. Arguments can be made in favor of a nation's need for, and use of, a royal family.

But when we think of Jesus... and the kind of world he envisions and calls us to help make real… should we look to monarchies to find Christian example? Of course, the answer more times than not is "no." And we have to answer in the negative because of the subtle distinction between the terms "power" and "authority."

In today's gospel lesson, Jesus teaches us that at the end of time, God will judge the nations of the world by how they treated persons who were most in need.

Nations need to be careful not to worship "power." Because when it is power we are after, we will have no problem dehumanizing and mistreating others to secure our own future. The thirst for power is rooted in fear. And while we see this posture often in Scripture, I find it most clear in the story of the twins Jacob and Esau.

Esau and Jacob were at odds with each other, not simply for much of their adult lives. Their wrestling began in their mother Rebekah's womb… their conflict was very much a part of who they were.

At birth, Esau came out first… and Jacob came out second, grabbing onto Esau. Jacob's name means "heel-grabber"... and rabbis tell us Jacob is symbolic of those who pull others down in order to raise up themselves.

Nations and people, when living in fear, act out of their insecurities… believing that to achieve their own good, they need to tear down others in the process. For me to succeed, you have to fail. For me to be empowered, you need to be powerless.

This is the way much of the world operates. But Jesus says this is not God's way. The nations of the world should not worship "power," but they do need to understand… and be responsible with… their "authority."

Nations who understand "authority" will go out of their way to, as Jesus says, feed the hungry… give drink to the thirsty… welcome the stranger… clothe the naked… heal the sick… and come to the side of those imprisoned.

Jesus says that when we minister with compassion toward people in these and other vulnerable conditions, it is the same as if we were ministering to him.

Now, I am not going to stand here and tell you I do perfectly or always what Jesus is saying. I get how difficult it is. I and other clergy struggle with the complexity of this truth… or maybe we make it out to be more difficult than it is because it is such a profound statement from Jesus.

It is too easy a solution for many who claim they want to experience God.

Jesus says that when we approach those in need and seek to help them... and not ignore them, or expel them, or judge them for not living up to the standards we set for them… we will discover Christ in them… we will encounter God directly.

***

Last Sunday afternoon, we had about 500 people in here for our Interfaith Service of Thanksgiving. 500. Standing room only.

I dare say that half of those in attendance are not Christians… and a significant number of the non-Christians are relatively new to the United States.

One of the things I learned in advance of last week's service is that when persons of other faiths encounter Christianity in America, it is often an experience of Christianity in "power." I am right. You are wrong. You need to change. And if you cannot deal with this, maybe you need to go back to where you're from.

The feedback I have received over the past week… well, even before… is that persons we invited into this House of Prayer learned that the people of St. John's love them. You love them. By extension, it is fair to say… and for others to understand... that Jesus loves them.

That is not Christian power.

That is Christian authority.

In Jesus, we have the authority to share God's love… and let the chips fall where they may.

I am so proud of, and inspired by, you the family of St. John's that you are secure enough in your devotion to Jesus that you can embody God's love for all.

May God give us the grace to continue being who we are… and communicate what it truly means for Christ to be King.

DECEMBER

Sleepwalking through Life

Homily for December 3, 2017

Today is the First Sunday of Advent, the Church's season of eager expectation. We highlight this transition with blue vestments... calming shades similar to what we notice in our sunrises and sunsets at this time of year.

We will recite Eucharistic Prayer B... offer a different form of the Prayers of the People... and count each Sunday lighting candles on the Advent wreath.

And in this new church year, we focus on readings from the Gospel according to Mark.

Each time the Church changes seasons, we put ourselves in a position to hear God afresh.

This Advent, even though Mark's gospel does not have any stories on the birth of Jesus, we still call to mind the way... and ways... God is born into our lives in this chaotic world.

It is not just the first coming of Christ from two thousand years ago which should get our attention... or the Second Coming the Church is called to anticipate, that reality when Christ will make all things new.

Advent reminds us how God, in Christ, through the power of the Holy Spirit enters our lives now to offer us that peace which the world cannot give.

***

While this morning's gospel lesson is about the Second Coming of Christ… there is a two-word phrase Jesus repeats which underscores the point of God coming close now.

Jesus says: keep alert… keep awake… keep awake.

One of the theologians I read a lot is a Catholic priest named Richard Rohr. For the sake of attribution, his work has shaped much of how I approach Jesus' words here.

If Jesus is telling us to keep awake, it is because there are good activities in our lives which… when we are not alert... can actually lull us to sleep. And when we consider waking or sleeping, we should not understand this necessarily in the literal sense. Think metaphorically and spiritually.

One question we need to consider in Advent is this: how much time do we spend sleepwalking through our lives?

***

I do not mean this in a bad way, because I am going to throw myself under the bus, too… but last week at church, we had a lot of people here. Yet we all had a Thanksgiving hangover.

Maybe there was still too much tryptophan from the turkey in our systems.

For many of us, the Thanksgiving break was the first time in a long time that we were able to take a few days off from work or school. We spent time with family or friends. We slept. We broke from the daily routine… and that impacted us physically and emotionally.

While we know the holidays are not enjoyable for all, there are times when a disruption to our busy schedules can work to our advantage.

In and of itself, there is nothing wrong with a full schedule. But there is a risk which comes from living in a culture that connects busy-ness to worthiness… activity to upward mobility.

When we are preoccupied with a non-critical approach to ambition, we miss out on what is truly important in life.

Parents sacrifice relationships with children on the altar of a successful business career. We trick ourselves into thinking that if we spend more time at the office, we automatically become better providers for our family. This is not true.

Nor is there complete truth in attempts to redefine "relationships" in the age of the internet. We now claim friendships by the number of persons who follow us on social media… instead of by the amount of face-to-face contact, in-depth discussion, and life-sharing we have with others.

Is it not possible for us to segregate ourselves on the web, interact solely with folks who are "like-minded" ... dehumanize those who do not think like we do… and then post online just the good things that happen in our lives... and not give the complete picture of who we are?

If we do not tell the full truth about ourselves to our so-called friends… or spend quality time with persons who hold different opinions on life's serious matters... do we really have "relationships?" Or are we connected only to catfishers, people who assume false identities online?

When we do engage on the person-to-person level, might we schedule every moment of our lives under the guise of being "involved"… tirelessly serving on community boards, coaching little league, or whatever the case may be?

Sure, we receive admiration for our commitment to serving others.

But do we lose ourselves in a way contrary to how Jesus calls us to lose ourselves?

Busy-ness for the sake of being busy puts us to sleep spiritually. It affords us the opportunity to suppress painful thoughts and feelings which surface each time we stumble upon quiet.

Mindless busy-ness helps us ignore pain which God desires to confront and transform.

When we define the "good life" by career, popularity, or a self-made trouble-free life... we may achieve short-term happiness when things go well. But there comes a time when a job, notoriety, or the pursuit of a "false peace" can no longer numb the hurts which need to be healed by God.

Sleepwalking through life gets us nowhere… which is why Advent says: wake up!

Wake up to the life-transforming power of God.

Wake up to the depth and integrity of relationship which God invites us to within the Church.

Wake up to Jesus, who is our facetime with God…heals our pain without diminishing it… and shows us the true nature of joy.

Wake up. Keep alert. Keep awake.

Expectation is Keepin' Me Waitin'

Homily for December 10, 2017

Last Sunday I mentioned how the season of Advent is the Church's time of "eager expectation."

"Eager expectation" is another way to say waiting.

Advent is about waiting, something I do not always do well in life's trivial matters. I am just plain bad at waiting for fast food... internet downloads... and the U-P-S driver.

Oh, the perils of First World Problems.

In a world of instant gratification, we have come to equate waiting not with eagerness, but anxiety… and out of anxiety… if we have to wait for longer than we want to wait, we look for someone to blame.

That is unfortunate… we need to know how to wait well… because, in many cases, waiting is important yet a difficult business.

Think about waiting for a medical diagnosis. A doctor or nurse notices particular symptoms, shares possibilities of the underlying issue with the patient, and then sends off bloodwork or x-rays to the lab for confirmation or denial.

Waiting for test results can take several days… if not longer… and for good reasons. There is a need for medical personnel to be thorough when it comes to our physical health and get things right.

But where do our minds go when we wait?

How do we attend to our spiritual health when we wait?

Waiting involves a degree of uncertainty… and in times of uncertainty, our minds can drive us down the road that leads to the worst-case scenario. And on that journey, we steer ourselves toward paths we hope will make us secure… less anxious. And there are times in our waiting when we make a wrong turn.

When we seek answers in times of uncertainty… but fail to do so biblically, prayerfully, and thoughtfully… we can get wrong what God desires to tell us in a particular moment.

We will project onto God elements we breathe in the culture… false notions of God.

How often do people try to get through the day by telling themselves that if they can just get on God's nice-list and stay off God's naughty-list, God will not punish them?

Nothing bad will happen to us so long as we are faithful, right?

In the immortal words of Janis Joplin:

Oh Lord, won't you buy me a Mercedes Benz ?

My friends all drive Porsches, I must make amends.

Worked hard all my lifetime, no help from my friends,

So Lord, won't you buy me a Mercedes Benz ?

Basing our lives on superstition leads us to believe that if we get a bad medical diagnosis… or do NOT get a prized possession... it is because God has declared us faithless, unworthy of God's love and blessing.

But that is not who God is.

God's relationship with humanity is not quid pro quo.

God's commitment to humanity is not predicated on humanity's faithfulness.

When difficult things happen in our lives… truly difficult things... instead of thinking we have done something to make God angry, and that simply amending our behavior will set things right again… we should use such opportunities to open ourselves to God, ask the tough questions in prayer… and wait.

Our Advent pondering then becomes: what does it mean to wait for a God who is faithful when we cannot always say the same about ourselves?

***

In this morning's Gospel lesson, Mark quotes the prophet Isaiah (40:3):

"See, I am sending my messenger ahead of you, who will prepare your way; the voice of one crying out in the wilderness: 'Prepare the way of the Lord, make his paths straight ...'"

Mark goes on to tell us that John the Baptist urged people to repent and be baptized.

Mark draws a connection between Isaiah's words and the presence and activity of John the Baptist.

Meaning, John the Baptist can teach us a thing or two about waiting for God in life's difficult moments.

John the Baptist says: ready or not, Jesus is coming… so let us get ready.

Are you with me?

John the Baptist does NOT say: Repent, and Jesus will come.

John says: Jesus is coming. Repent!

The nuance we need to understand is this:

Advent waiting is NOT about what we can do to perfect our lives and make Christ come.

Advent waiting is about how we are to be... how we are to live our lives... SINCE Christ is coming.

God is coming.

God is always faithful… so we have to ask the Advent questions differently:

How should we be when God does come?

And why not be that way now… before God comes?

If Jesus were present right now in human form… how would our thinking and our priorities need to change?

How would Jesus' immediate presence inform the way we treat each other… even in light of troubling interactions of the past?

How might Jesus' perspective on eternity, informed by the Cross and Resurrection, impact the way we think about our own physical ailments… and inevitable mortality?

Advent says God is coming to us in Jesus… so why not go ahead, in Advent and beyond, and live as if Christ has already come?

The Empty Tomb and the Manger

Homily for December 17, 2017

I want to spend a few moments identifying what some might call an elephant in the middle of the room, one of those things we know is there. But we hesitate to talk about it because, maybe, we think we are the only ones who see this elephant… or it is not polite to discuss it... or the elephant is just too painful for words.

When we get in our cars and turn on the radio, we are bombarded with Andy Williams crooning that it is the most wonderful time of the year. But for some, no, this is not the most wonderful time of the year.

This may be the first holiday season without a loved one. We are at the beginning of grieving that loved one's death. And we do not know how to process the endless flood of memories, and the emotions which come with them.

Or, it may have been many years since the death of someone we love… and through no fault of our own, the intensity of grief has not diminished. The wound is as deep and painful as the moment it was inflicted.

Grieving comes, too, with relational separation, divorce, estrangement, the loss of a job… watershed moments which prompt us to consider what gives meaning to our lives, our self-worth, whom and what we love, and whether or not we think we are lovable.

So when the expectation to have a holly jolly Christmas comes face-to-face with personal tragedy, we might wonder if we are doing something wrong.

But we are not.

Then we turn to God and the Church for comfort.

And we are startled by words of the Apostle Paul which make us question whether God and the Scriptures are tone deaf to our suffering.

But they are not.

Paul writes to persecuted, distressed, anxious Christians in Thessalonica (a city in Greece). He says:

"Rejoice always, pray without ceasing, give thanks in all circumstances; for this is the will of God in Christ Jesus for you." (1 Thessalonians 5:16)

Rejoice always?

Pray without ceasing?

Give thanks in all circumstances?

***

As we think about what it means to rejoice always, I could go into a long explanation about the difference between joy and happiness... and maybe talk about the depth of joy we find in Jesus, and how that is different from a surface feeling of happiness.

I could paint a picture of what it means to pray without ceasing... which is not a call to spend every moment alone, on our knees, and reciting the *Daily Office* in hopes of alleviating our pain.

No, praying without ceasing includes the posture of being awake and aware... as we examined on the First Sunday of Advent. "Being awake" spiritually is prayerful communication with God, in and of itself.

We could open our elementary school primers and focus on the power of prepositions… how the Apostle Paul does *not* exhort us to give thanks *for* all circumstances, but to give thanks *in* all circumstances.

We are not thankful to God for all that life has thrown our way.

And let me be clear. When something goes wrong, God is not the cause of our suffering.

Our suffering is the logical consequence of life in a world separated from God by the sin of Adam and Eve.

When we awaken to this distinction, we can then work on being thankful to God IN all things… even when life turns on a dime.

How in the world are we supposed to do that?

When life goes wrong, it is easy to close ourselves off from God's message in Jesus.

But as challenging as it is to hear and do… healing comes when we allow God to lead our wounded lives into the cave where Jesus was buried, and recall the cave where Jesus was born.

***

Like Mary Magdalene, when we approach the cave of death… the location of our deepest pain… we discover in faith that ultimately the tomb is empty.

In the Resurrection of Jesus, God overcomes the worst life can throw at us… the Holy Spirit orchestrates birth in the dark places of our lives.

This truth is why we are here in the first place… it is the foundation for thanksgiving in all things.

***

When Paul says rejoice always, pray without ceasing, give thanks in all circumstances… this is NOT a formula to magically make things better.

The Christian life does not work that way.

I do not want to give the impression that the healing of Christ will be instant, without its peaks and valleys… or will achieve its fullness in this life.

Paul writes these words… and the Church in her wisdom brings them to the fore…. because they point to a cascade of light in the darkest, coldest times of our lives.

Paul's words are not glib, intended to belittle our pain.

Rather, the white space surrounding the letters on the page invite us to pencil-in the depth of our suffering… and spell out the name of Jesus, the God who becomes like you and me to personally attend to our inmost needs.

As we continue our Advent path to the cave beneath the inn where there was no room for MARY and JOSEPH… may we have the grace to be honest about our grief… and trust God to empty the Tomb so it can be filled with the Manger.

An Advent "Fast Pass"

Homily for December 24, 2017

Today can be a peculiar day, but only if we allow it to be. It is the Fourth Sunday of Advent... and December 24, Christmas Eve.

The calendar has given us a Fast Pass to skip the final week of Advent... and move to the front of the line, which begins its queue outside the stable where the Christ-child is born.

We are presented with the gift of not having to wait for Christmas any longer than necessary.

But is this really a gift?

It is tempting to want to allow our minds to wander... and give in to thoughts which center our attentions on all that needs to be done today: last minute shopping, cooking, which Christmas Eve service to attend.

But as disciples of Jesus Christ... we must instead discipline ourselves for these few hours of the Fourth Sunday of Advent.

Instead of focusing on the "next thing" ... an ever-present temptation in our culture... can we take a deep breath, and focus on the present moment?

Can we give undivided attention and critical thought to what and who are right in front of us?

***

As we consider this morning's gospel passage, I invite you to call to mind someone you know who is almost 13-years-old. It may be a daughter or son, niece or nephew, grandchild, someone at St. John's or in your neighborhood.

The young woman we are introduced to in this section of Luke's gospel is the same age as the person you have brought to mind.

And as we get to know Mary, we learn she is betrothed to a man named Joseph... who was likely much older than she.

It was not uncommon for Jewish girls of that day to be betrothed at what we consider a tender age.

Betrothal was a deep commitment… which we compare and contrast to our understanding of engagement.

Mary and Joseph, at this point in their relationship, did not live together.

According to the terms of betrothal, the bride-to-be would still live with her parents for about one year before the wedding ceremony.

For all intents and purposes, the couple was looked upon as married… but with betrothal, they would not take part in marital relations.

I wonder how Mary anticipated her wedding day… if she ever got caught up in some of the things young couples do today … if she agonized over the guest list… or wondered who would cater the reception.

Did Mary dream about how many children she and Joseph would have? What names would they bestow on their children?

I do not think it is too much of a stretch to believe, in a non-academic/non-theological sense, that Mary did have plans for her life with Joseph.

But as we know in our day, there is a popular, Yiddish proverb which says: when we make plans, God laughs.

In Mary's case, it might be better to quote the Book of Proverbs (19:21): "Many are the plans in a person's heart, but it is the LORD's purpose that prevails."

The angel Gabriel comes to inform Mary of God's purpose for her life.

God chose to become human by way of Mary's womb.

Mary was to be the Mother of God, to birth Jesus to the world.

Some stumble on the notion that Mary could become pregnant through the overshadowing of the Holy Spirit… instead of by Joseph or anyone else.

Some refuse to believe God could interact with the material world in such a way.

But I count myself among the multitude who have no trouble believing in the Virginal Conception of Jesus… and notice I did NOT say Immaculate Conception.

The Immaculate Conception is a Roman Catholic dogma which puts forth the notion that Mary was free from the stain of original sin when she was conceived. It has nothing to do with what we are talking about here in Luke's gospel.

It is the Virginal Conception which applies to Jesus… and I do not have to cross my fingers when we recite this line in the Nicene and Apostles' Creeds.

If God can create the entire universe, what's the big deal with the conception of the Christ-child through the power of the Holy Spirit?

***

To me, I marvel at Mary's faith… I am struck by Mary's ability to give undivided attention and critical thought to the angel of the Lord… her discipline to be in the moment with God.

When Gabriel tells Mary of God's purpose for her life, she immediately gives priority to the LORD's plan over her own.

Mary says "yes" to the angel… "yes" to God… even though she likely knew it could jeopardize her pending marriage to Joseph.

It did not.

Mary says "yes" to God… even though people in her village then, and people now, would doubt her story… and they would, in turn, look down their noses at Mary and gossip.

They did. They do.

People might have doubted Mary… but that did not sway Mary because she never doubted God for one moment.

So when Mary questions Gabriel about God's plan, this is not evidence of disbelief on Mary's part. No, Mary is simply curious about procedure.

When God calls on Mary to give birth to the savior of the world, her question is not a cynical "are you kidding me?"

Mary's question is: "Lord, how are you going to make this happen through me?"

Mary had enough history with God to know that God is trustworthy.

Her question had nothing to do with whether or not God would be faithful.

Mary… as part of her acceptance of God's will... simply wanted to know God's game plan.

Can we say the same about our own relationship with God?

When God calls us to bear Christ to the world in our own way, have we immersed ourselves enough in Word and Sacrament to know that God is faithful?

Do we give too much attention to what others might think?

Do we worry how God's plan might inconvenience us?

Or, when considering God's faithfulness to Mary by sending the Christ-child into her life… can we trust God enough to say: "... let it be to me according to your word."

Angels We Have "Herd" on High

Homily for Christmas Eve 2017

It is an honor and a privilege to celebrate the birth of the Christ-child with you tonight, my first Nativity Feast as your rector.

It is also the first Christmas in many years that Margaret, Karina, Cade, and I have been able to hang stockings by a fireplace.

And it is not just four stockings we put up.

No, break out M.C. Hammer and the Command Hooks, the Normans have eight stockings above our fireplace.

Yes, eight.

As in 1-2-3-4-5-6-7-8!

Don't get any ideas. There will not be any more births into the Norman family.

No, we have four cats.

The minister's cats are a-numerous cats… and they are named Stripey, Elvis, Callie, and JJ.

Stripey is a tabby with gray and black stripes. Hence, Stripey.

Elvis is all black… and when we adopted him we somehow made a connection with Elvis Presley. And, no, this cat does not have blue suede paws.

Callie is a calico. Not too much originality there, I know.

And then there is JJ. … JJ Redick Norman.

When JJ was born in the bushes outside our house in Texas, I promised the family we would take him in only if we could name him after my favorite basketball player:

JJ Redick, a Duke University graduate, 12th year in the National Basketball Association, now with the Philadelphia 76ers.

Here's the thing about the four Norman cats.

Elvis gravitates toward Karina… but tolerates the rest of us. Elvis meows woefully at humans when we sit in what apparently is his recliner in the living room.

Stripey is loving to all… but not the brightest creature God has ever made. Every night, Stripey attempts to sleep on Margaret's head… and every night, he fails.

Callie is 100-percent my cat… she keeps me company wherever I am in the house. And like any good mother, although she has never had kittens, Callie is protective of all humans and animals in our home.

JJ is pretty much still a kitten… a third teenager in the house. He has perfected the art of eating needles off our Christmas tree… and returning them in recognizable form to areas near and far from the tree.

If we cannot find JJ in the house, we know to look in Cade's room… JJ is either sleeping on Cade's bed, or stretched out beneath Cade's drumset.

Our cats have distinct personalities… and preferred humans.

But when these four cats are hungry, they go to one person.

They gather at the side of this person's bed at 4am… pawing at said person's head… or climbing over… or starting a fight with each other because this one human will awaken, throw in their general direction a premium "My Pillow" manufactured in Minnesota by Michael Lindell... and beg them to stop.

Guess who that human is?

Me.

There are three other humans in the house!

But when these four cats want to be fed… if there is plenty of food in their bowls but they can still see the bottom of their bowls... they come to me!

Why, Lord?!?

There was one Saturday morning when Margaret had to get up early to take Cade to a school event. She tried to lead the cats down the stairs to feed them.

But they would not go.

The cats waited until I was awake to gallup to their food bowls in the kitchen.

Those cats have trained me well.

They own me.

Never mind the phrase "herding cats."

Those four cats herd me.

***

In our gospel lesson on this holy night, there is a whole lot of herding going on.

The most obvious herding takes place with Luke's mention of shepherds in a field, guarding their flocks by night.

Such herding calls to mind images of the Good Shepherd in the 23rd Psalm… one who brings abundance, peace, restoration, and comfort.

When the angel tells these shepherds of the birth of the Christ-child, they make haste to guide themselves and their sheep to Jesus.

It is a beautiful form of herding.

***

A second, and somewhat less obvious example of herding is carried out by the Roman Emperor Augustus… at the time Syria was administered by someone named Quirinius.

The Roman government occupied the Jewish homeland… and was herding the Jewish people under their rule… ordering the populace to their hometowns to be counted for taxation.

Roman government officials… shepherds of a self-serving herd… were as oblivious as sheep when it came to empathy toward their Jewish subjects.

Their herding was done not for the peace, restoration, or comfort of the powerless… it was to increase the excess of those already in power.

***

The signature example of herding in tonight's gospel passage comes at the initiative of God.

On this night, we are reminded that the Lord truly is our Shepherd… who desires to guide us to places of abundance, peace, restoration, and comfort.

When Jesus is born into the chaotic, divided reality we are tempted to accept as the "new normal" … He is God drawing us close… He is God herding us.

The infant Jesus is God… weak and vulnerable... overturning the ways of life which benefit the dominant at the expense of the disenfranchised.

***

When our souls have their fill of what the world too easily accepts as the "new normal"… we reach for an animal's feeding trough which cradles the Christ-child.

The manger endows us with the God who gives us resolve to unfollow the wrong herd… and be guided in God's herd of Love.

Receive the good news of great joy for all the people … to us is born this night a Savior, who is the Messiah, the Lord.

May we all have a Merry Christmas.

The Gift

Meditation for Christmas Day 2017

Good morning and Merry Christmas!

I do not need to see a show of hands, or anything like that. But I am curious.

For those of you with children and/or grandchildren at your homes this holiday, how much sleep did you get last night? How early did the young children… or even older children… roust you out of bed so that they could open their presents?

It is an exciting morning to be sure… the fulfillment of wishes long hoped for.

The receiving of gifts.

The utter demolition of wrapping paper.

Not one gift left under a tree or in its box.

Gratitude toward the giver of gifts.

Today we commemorate God's gift to all of humanity… all the world… and the entire cosmos, in the person of Jesus of Nazareth… God coming to us in humility, as an infant, entering the world the same as we did.

While it is important to note that in Jesus' adult life, death, and resurrection, he bridges the gap which seeks to separate humanity from God… we pause to consider the fact that the God who created all there is thinks so highly of us that this God became one of us.

God, born as Jesus, validates our humanity… shows us that “matter matters” (N.T. Wright) … the material world is not inherently evil, but is declared “good” by God.

Everything about the core essence of who we are as a human being is legitimized in the birth of Christ Jesus.

He is God’s gift to us.

But here’s the thing about a gift.

It is important that God sends us the gift of Himself in Jesus.

But it is equally important that we receive the gift of Jesus into our lives.

When the shepherds were told by the angel Gabriel about the birth of Jesus, they rushed to the manger with the same excitement and urgency many children had early this morning... as they made their way to the gifts they knew awaited them.

And like any other gift, God’s gift of Jesus has to be opened… we have to work our way through the wrapping, baggage which may conceal his beauty and purpose… cloaking his importance in our lives.

And, like all other gifts, Jesus is not for admiration only. We are to (figuratively speaking) take Jesus out of the box, and put him to use… integrate the gift of God into our everyday lives.

This morning, and every day of your lives… God offers a most precious gift in Jesus… and the packaging around this gift has your name on it… He is for you.

May we all have the grace to receive the gift of the Christ-child… and have a very Merry Christmas.

A New Year's Resolve

December 31, 2017

Today is one of those days when we are keenly aware of voices which call into question our self-image.

It is New Year's Eve on the secular calendar. And we are, in various ways, shamed into making New Year's resolutions.

What are we going to do differently in 2018?

How might we change our appearance?

How can we adjust our habits in such a way for others to think more highly of us?

There are plenty of commercials which promise that by the middle of February, we will have successfully lost weight… be more confident in our buff bodies… and no longer have the urge to smoke. Or whatever.

Make yourself more attractive to whoever it is you want to find you attractive.

If a product marketed for external transformation does not suit your fancy, try spending one dollar a minute on the telephone with a psychic. Nothing says "Happy New Year" like a vague conversation with an unseen stranger about your future.

But I know from previous New Year's resolutions, no matter how much money I spend on a miracle product, I will have broken my promise to myself by the middle of next week.

What happens to the "motivation" I feel when staying up late watching the crowd in Times Square?

Pills and potions which promise a quick-fix… or charming, hollow words from a charlatan... are not long-term solutions for our lives, if they can even be called solutions.

We know we must dig deeper.

As we consider the persistent tug to be what some might call better versions of ourselves, we need to ask the question: whose love and affirmation do we seek?

This question is not limited to a new calendar year. It is a question we, as followers of Jesus, should ask daily.

Whose love and affirmation do we seek?

***

This morning's Gospel passage comes from our patron, St. John. His prologue is considered by many theologians to be one of the most beautiful pieces of literature ever.

John's is a highly theologized account of Jesus… distinct from the synoptic gospels: Matthew, Mark, and Luke. And we notice this with John's first words.

Mark begins his book with the Baptism of Jesus. There is mention of a different John, the Baptizer, and we meet Jesus as an adult.

Matthew and Luke start theirs with stories centered on the birth of Jesus.

Matthew centers on Joseph, the adoptive father of Jesus.

Luke shares with us visitations of the angel Gabriel's interactions... first to the parents of John the Baptizer... and then to Mary, the mother of Jesus.

But John is different.

What John wants us to realize... without discounting the other gospel writers... is that God's plan for humanity in Jesus was initiated NOT when Jesus was baptized at age 30... or when the angel of the Lord appeared to Mary right before Jesus was conceived.

No, God's plan for humanity in Jesus was in place at the foundation of everything.

John writes: "In the beginning was the Word, and the Word was with God, and the Word was God. He was in the beginning with God. All things came into being through him, and without him not one thing came into being." (John 1:1-3)

When we hear the phrase "In the beginning" ... our minds are taken, rightly so, to the opening lines of the Book of Genesis, the moment when God created all there is, bringing order out of chaos, pushing back the darkness with light.

John tells us that the Word... in Greek the "Logos"... what retired Pope Benedict XVI calls the "creative reason"[8] which undergirds all of life... the Christ was there at the beginning of all things. And it was through this Word, this Logos, this Christ, that all things came into being.

The Christ, the Second Person of the Trinity, became human... like us... in the person of Jesus of Nazareth.

For longer than we can fathom and imagine, God's plan was, is, and shall be to **dwell** with humanity... to be with you... to be with me... and draw us deeply into the life God desires for us.

---

[8] Pope Benedict XVI - *Jesus of Nazareth: The Infancy Narratives*

So when we are encouraged to make New Year's resolutions because we fail to measure up to a particular, subjective, cultural standard… we simply need to recall how God felt about us at the very beginning. It is the same way God feels about us now… a fact we know from Jesus.

God loves us… God bestows a dignity on us in Jesus in ways we cannot acquire by our own means.

Jesus is the only AFFIRMATION we need… the only MOTIVATION we need as we begin a new year... because Jesus is forever God's New Life Resolution.

INDEX

INDEX

About the Author

The Reverend Curt Norman began his ministry at St. John's on January 8, 2017.

Father Curt received his Bachelor of Arts in Radio, Television and Film from the University of North Texas (Denton, Texas) and his Master of Divinity from the University of the South School of Theology (Sewanee, Tennessee) in 2001. He served as Curate at Christ Church – Plano, Texas; Associate Rector at St. Peter's – Del Mar, California; and Associate Rector at Holy Faith – Santa Fe, New Mexico. Prior to arriving in Saginaw, Father Curt served as Rector of St. Luke's – Denison, Texas; and Rector of St. Luke's – Stephenville, Texas.

Curt is married to Margaret Link Norman. They have two children, Karina and Cade.

Reviews

Curt Norman sets out to preach a political Gospel beyond partisans in a deeply partisan age. In a year's worth of sermons - both deeply personal to the community to which he's preaching and widely applicable to many settings - Norman displays a deep love for the Scriptures, for the people he serves, and for the God he worships. From sports analogies to deeply theological reflection to historical minutiae, he weaves together an impressive breadth of knowledge with succinctness and clarity. These sermons from a rector's first year in a new place in a divided time offer a perspective of hope for the future of the Church, and for the already-but-not-yet reign of God.

The Rev. Jordan Haynie Ware, author of *The Ultimate Quest: A Geek's Guide to (the Episcopal) Church* and priest in the Anglican Church of Canada.

***

Because I have known Curt since early in his priestly ministry, it is a great joy to see how he has grown into an excellent preacher and priest. His sermons are strongly grounded in good Biblical scholarship, in a mature theology and an obvious deep love for his congregation. After reading this collection, it is apparent that his gift to the congregation goes well beyond homiletics, to the more important gift --- himself.

The Rev. Canon Stephen H. Wendfeldt

***

Making All Things New in Old Town is a delightful peek inside the life of an Episcopal congregation in 2017. Curt preaches a broad and loving theology as he reminds us all that God is present and very involved in our day to day hopes and dreams, even as God also hopes and dreams we will change the world in our own small corners of it.

The Rev. Amy Haynie, Clergy Associate, Trinity Episcopal Church, Ft Worth, TX

***

Curt cuts through the din of cultural noise to proclaim the Gospel of Jesus Christ to us in and to our present context. He doesn't shrink from expressing what so many think, but won't address, even when it is his own struggle. Curt's is a refreshing voice reminding us not only who God is, but also who we are.

The Rev. Canon P. Lance Ousley, Canon for Stewardship and Development,
Diocese of Olympia (WA) and
Priest in Charge, St. John Episcopal Church, Kirkland, WA.

***

In Curtis Norman's *Making All Things New in Old Town*, we encounter the homilies of an Episcopal Priest who consistently invites and encourages those with whom he shares community to consider: "Who Jesus is?" "Who we are?" "And how our responses to the aforementioned queries inform how we relate to ourselves, one another and our world." If these queries resonate, and I hope they do, please read on...

The Right Reverend David Rice, Bishop
The Episcopal Diocese of San Joaquin

***

I have known Curt for 30 years and during this time watched him struggle with the issues of life and the Church. Above all I have watched him keep his focus on those issues which truly matter in his life and the life of the people he serves and preach to those issue. This collection of sermons shows his intellectual curiosity, passion and respect for his listeners as both he and they learn anew what it means to be part of the Body of Christ.

The Rev. Canon David W. Holland, TSSF

CPSIA information can be obtained
at www.ICGtesting.com
Printed in the USA
BVHW04*1057170918
527708BV00014B/1341/P

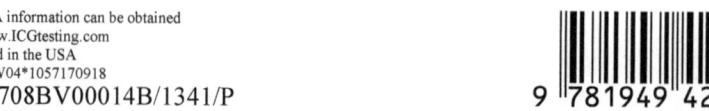